# SLAPHAPPY

# SLAP HAPPY

## PRIDE, PREJUDICE, & PROFESSIONAL WRESTLING

WITH PHOTOGRAPHS BY THE AUTHOR

# THOMAS HACKETT

ecco
ANNIVERSARY
35

HarperCollins books may be purchased for educational, business, or sales promotional use. For information please write: Special Markets Department, HarperCollins Publishers, 10 East 53rd Street, New York, NY 10022.

FIRST EDITION

*Designed by Judith Stagnitto Abbate/Abbate Design*

Library of Congress Cataloging-in-Publication Data

Hacket, Thomas.
  Slaphappy : pride, prejudice, and professional wrestling / Thomas Hackett.
    p.  cm.
  ISBN-10: 0-06-019829-X
  ISBN-13: 978-0-06-019829-9
    1. Wrestling.  2. Wrestling—Social aspects.  I. Title: Slaphappy.
  II. Title.
  GV1195.H23 2006
  796.812—dc22

                                                          2005049493

06  07  08  09  10  BVG/RRD  10  9  8  7  6  5  4  3  2  1

TO MY MOTHER

# ACKNOWLEDGMENTS

T HANKS TO the hundreds of fans who eagerly shared their passion for professional wrestling with me, particularly Urial Yakobov; to the dozens of wrestlers who may have bridled at my pesky questions but answered them anyway, Oren Hawxhurst especially; to professors Ted Friedman, Michael Hackett, Wayne Koestenbaum, Toby Miller, Gillian Silverman, Robert Thompson, and the brilliant Jay Fliegelman for their insights into popular American culture; to Calpernia Addams, Bob Barnett, Barry Blaustein, John Dolin, J. Michael Kenyon, Chuck Palahniuk, and especially Susan Faludi for *their* insights; to Rob Grover, my sure-handed editor at Ecco, to Ed Cohen, for his careful copyediting, and Judith Stagnitto Abbate for her cool design; to Dan Halpern, David Halpern, and David McCormick for their guidance and patience; to Russ

Hoyle, Ed Kosner, and Bob Sapio at the New York *Daily News*; to my friends Nancy Franklin, Pascale LeDraoulec, Becky Ogburn, and especially Bruce Diones and Marc Weingarten, for advice and much more; and to my parents and my sisters, particularly Mollie, an astute first reader. Finally, I want to single out Thomas Healy for help above and beyond the call of friendship.

# CONTENTS

# SLAPHAPPY

# INTRODUCTION

THE ENTIRE SPECTACLE IS BEFORE US. WE HAVE
ONLY TO READ IT, STUDY ITS CONSTANT PAT-
TERNS, ANALYZE ITS VARIATIONS.

—JOSEPH CAMPBELL

N LAS VEGAS a few years ago, at the annual meeting of the Cauliflower Alley
Club—a group of old-time professional
wrestlers and their fans—I met a thirty-
three-year-old man who called himself
The Almighty Ultimate. He carried
himself with a serene self-confidence
and, despite a flabby belly, pigeon chest, and
spindly arms, claimed to be a professional
wrestler. He was quite possibly stoned out of
his gourd. "Use marijuana and prosper" was
the first thing he said to me. The Almighty
Ultimate went on to say that he had wrestled
Stone Cold Steve Austin professionally in
1979 (when they would have been ten and

1

fifteen years old, respectively), that at the time he had been a midget wrestler, that he would now be the undisputed world champion if Ric "Nature Boy" Flair had not broken into his house and hypnotized him, that he was related to a Zulu chief, and, finally, that he suffered from gigantism. "I've got a kind of bone and muscle structure that enables me to transform myself, to get taller and bigger at will," he explained. "Right now, my head's expanding."

The Almighty Ultimate was the laughingstock of the gathering. It occurred to me, though, that perhaps he was not out of his mind—that maybe he had taken a page from the comedian Andy Kaufman, who perpetrated one of the best "works" in wrestling history, as the World Intergender Champion. Kaufman's friends and managers desperately wished that he'd drop the wrestling shtick; it wasn't funny, they complained. But Kaufman was not going for laughs. All that really interested him was people asking: "Is this guy for real?" And maybe that was what this man who bragged that he had won "Mr. Gargantuan" and "Smartest Man in the World" competitions was up to that weekend in Las Vegas, as well.

The Almighty Ultimate was just one of the hundreds of odd lost souls I met while researching this book. I have thought a lot about him, though. Whatever professional wrestling is about—and at the time of our meeting, I had only the vaguest idea of what that might be—it seemed to me that it was concerned with the kinds of questions that people like The Almighty Ultimate raised. He might, or might not, have known that he wasn't "for real," important to nobody as a performer, except, of course, to himself. But what did "real" mean, anyway? And what did it matter?

These, it seemed to me, were questions worth asking not just of professional wrestling, but also of American culture.

I suspect that anyone who delves into a subculture, be it baseball or Barbies, starts to see evidence of its sensibility everywhere he looks. I certainly did when I began hanging out with professional wrestlers and their fans. I don't only mean the easy jokes people made, comparing a political debate, say, to the posturing of a wrestling match. I mean the ways in which it seemed only natural, and therefore unremarkable, that American culture should operate according to the berserk logic of professional wrestling.

An entirely too willing suspension of disbelief—of enthusiastically accepting something we knew to be false or fictional as true or real—was the operative principle here. Even before the stock market crashed in February 2000, for example, investors understood that the soaring value of hundreds of publicly traded companies had almost nothing to do with their earnings; it was a pretend prosperity that could be sustained only so long as everyone bought into the fantasy. And why shouldn't they? In less than six months, a fifteen-year-old kid made more than $800,000 playing the stock market like a video game. He would buy stocks and then, using lots of capital letters and exclamation points, he'd tout their growth potential in hundreds of Internet postings. As soon as the credulous started buying, he'd sell, turning a nifty profit. Not coincidentally, the kid was a pro wrestling fan, and from it he'd learned a valuable lesson: nobody minds a con.

I am tempted to give other examples (the presidency of George W. Bush has provided plenty of them), but this book isn't about business, politics, or any of the other areas of public life that traffic in untruths. It's about pro wrestling, a subject easy to criticize in its own right. Violent, perverse, sexist, stupid . . . paradoxically, one thing wrestling *isn't* is dishonest. Although the wrestlers are playing pretend, wrestling itself does not pretend to be anything other than what it is—fantastically absurd. At the best live shows, you enter a euphoria of utter absurdity, and to analyze and interpret risks spoiling the pleasures of watching vivacious young men momentarily escaping civilization's discontents (not to mention their own). Unlike other forms of performance art, wrestling seems altogether insensible to Matthew Arnold's definition of culture—"the best that man has thought and known." Even at its best, at its most inspired, wrestling could never be anything other than stupendously bad.

Or so I thought.

"Everything fucking means something!" I once heard one of my favorite wrestlers tell some rookies backstage at a show in Philadelphia. A notorious drunk, he had just finished off a half-gallon of vodka; in a few minutes he would vomit all over the locker-room floor, then pass out in front of his wife and kids. The speech was impressive, however. Every match, he explained, was made up of about twenty choreographed moves, called "spots"; at every juncture, a wrestler had about eight choices, he figured. You could do an arm drag, a wrist-lock, a suplex . . . "Think about it—that's eight to the power of twenty . . . that's—" He threw out a sufficiently large number. "That's how many fucking choices you have! And you have to find the right ones, because they all fucking mean something!"

Although I can't vouch for his math, I think he's basically right. The object of art and culture is "to invent a vocabulary and a language by which man is able to externalize and project his inner states," says the cultural historian Lewis Mumford.

Professional wrestling may do this less elegantly and imaginatively than other types of theatrical performance. It may seem idiotic and incomprehensible to many people. It may lack conceptual clarity. But for a fan, I think wrestling gives "concrete and public form to his emotions, his feelings, his intuitions," to use Mumford's words. For the wrestlers, the rituals effectively dramatize their struggles to measure up to what society considers success. And that being a difficult question, wrestling offers no easy answers. On the surface, it seems to present a simplistic view of life, with good guys and bad guys, babyfaces and heels, representing clear examples of right and wrong. But the total effect of its never-ending narrative says something far more ambiguous and complex.

The more wrestling I watched, the more I was forced to acknowledge that wrestling had to be about . . . something. Something about men, about sex, about shame, about honor, about power, about status, about celebrity . . . something about America. The Almighty Ultimate personified those preoccupations. If he was mad—and anyone claiming to be a stand-in for both Henry Kissinger and the band Kiss would seem so—it was a very American kind of madness. Celebrity obsessed, pathologically narcissistic, murderously competitive . . . professional wrestling both epitomized and parodied the delusional egoism at the heart of the culture.

Aficionados will point out that wrestling exists all over the world, from the sumo giants of Japan to the gymnastic luchadors of Mexico to the regal Nubas of Sudan. Wrestling is perhaps man's oldest living language, preceding even speech. But while the sport may not be distinctly American, its unabashedly exhibitionistic, egomaniacal rituals are.

Professional wrestling, I came to believe, is us.

**4**

# CHAPTER ONE

OUR WHOLE LIFE IS LIKE A PLAY: WHEREIN
EVERY MAN FORGETFUL OF HIMSELF IS IN TRA-
VAIL WITH EXPRESSION OF ANOTHER. . . .
THOUGH THE MOST BE PLAYERS, SOME MUST
BE SPECTATORS.              —BEN JONSON

L ET ME ASK you something," said Joe
Joe Russello, Jr., age eleven, interrupting a conversation I was having
with his father. "How can you write
a book on something you don't
know shit about?"

"Well . . ." I started.

"Because either you got the balls of a
fucking lion, asking a bunch of bullshit questions," he said, jabbing a finger in my face as
his father looked on proudly, "or you've got
problems."

Joe Joe had a point. Sitting in my Man-

FACING: JOE JOE RUSSELLO, JR.                    7

hattan apartment, I had developed a lot of fancy theories about professional wrestling. I had gone to quite a few shows, yet always in the same spirit I had crashing debutante balls, cult gatherings, and Ku Klux Klan marches—to smirk and sneer. Channel surfing, I'd stop on the wrestling broadcasts long enough to feel superior. Maybe I just didn't get it, though. Those tribal rituals you see on PBS, where swaybacked savages dance about shamelessly naked, have always seemed pretty ridiculous, too. There was that reverent voice-over, however, explaining how the seeming imbecilities of the tribal rite contained and communicated everything that mattered to its culture. Perhaps professional wrestling was a story that we, too, were telling ourselves about ourselves.

At the very least it was a popular story. In 2001, at the height of its recent resurgence, nearly 15 percent of the population considered themselves fans, and the industry was making more than $450 million a year. Finding renewed interest every five or ten years, pro wrestling has been a mainstay of American popular culture for over a century. It wasn't quite the cult phenomenon it had been in 1985, when Cyndi Lauper, Liberace, and Robert Goulet made appearances at the first WrestleMania at New York's Madison Square Garden, or that it was in 1987, for WrestleMania III, when the Pontiac Silverdome in Detroit hosted the largest indoor gathering in the history of the human race, at least according to organizers. And despite the energetic marketing of stars like Stone Cold Steve Austin and The Rock, no rivalry yet equaled the 1911 fight in Chicago's Comiskey Park between Frank Gotch and George Hackenschmidt—a front-page story across the country. But in a brave new world of dot-coms, instant global communications, and human cloning, the premodern throwback of wrestling was once again a force to be reckoned with, and its fans could no longer be dismissed as credulous bumpkins caught up in vaguely pornographic pleasures. They now constituted a formidable demographic. "We are the voice of the people," said Linda McMahon, chief executive officer of World Wrestling Entertainment (WWE). Coming up on the 2000 presidential election, Linda's husband, Vince McMahon, Jr., was telling his followers that they, "the average wrestling fan," would elect the next president of the United States. And the thing is, he was not completely wrong.

That wasn't wrestling's only relevance to politics. As far as I could tell, both were part and parcel of the same culture of unreality. To reckon with wrestling, in other words, was to reckon with our cultural pathologies in a time of extravagant public inanity.

It was in that environment that millions of young men, in an effort to understand what success and masculinity were all about in America, turned to the culture's most grotesque example of ego and ambition. What they learned wasn't always very encouraging. With an abundance of enthusiasm, boys set out to reinvent themselves as models of manliness. They hoped to defeat insecurities, discover forgotten powers, and show the world they mattered. A few succeeded, rather spectacularly. But all too often the journey led to new insecurities, new fears. Getting caught up in the swirl of celebrity and status, they fell into some disorienting ironies. To prove their strength, they played the victim. To seem macho, they became dandies. To assert their heterosexuality, they acted out homoerotic skits. The fact that all these ironies were right there on the surface and yet could be acknowledged only in the most roundabout way was what made the spectacle so fascinating.

But it was also what made wrestling so bewildering, for the wrestlers especially.

I wanted to try to untangle that confusion. First, though, I had to understand why wrestling meant so much to so many people. What did it say to them? What did it say *for* them? And what did it say about the rest of us?

My first serious attempts to find out were not successful. For a couple of weeks I followed Ted Turner's World Championship Wrestling (WCW) around the state of Texas. I went to shows in Amarillo, Abilene, Waco, Beaumont, Houston, and San Padre Island—at least, I'm pretty sure I did. My travels in Texas are now a blur, but, alas, not of the debauched drugs-and-hookers, fear-and-loathing variety. It was a blur of dumbfounding boredom. Whether it was a house show or a television taping, every match repeated the same undifferentiated routine. Wrestlers made their self-important entrances, threw each other around in a kind of bullying ballet until they and the referee perfunctorily brought the acrobatics to a summary conclusion, at which point they would leave the ring either exultant or shamefaced. Watching on TV, you at least had the benefit of histrionic ringside announcers injecting the antics full of dire meaning. Live, it all just seemed an elaborate demonstration of pointlessness.

Long after I left Texas, though, I found myself thinking about the fans I had met. Fans like Frenchie, an elderly convenience-store clerk, and his young girlfriend, Dee, a nude dancer at Cloud Nine Cabaret; Melanie and Ryan Bernard, ages nineteen and twenty-one, who, instead of exchanging rings at their recent wedding, exchanged those bright and brassy belts that wrestlers wore; the middle-aged brother and sister who brought a poodle to a show, saying it was their daughter; and Bernice and Beulah, the pleasantly plump spinster sisters in matching appliqué sweatshirts, who maintained a website in memory of fellow Texan and former National Wrestling Alliance champion Kerry Von Erich.

When talking to wrestlers, I had to play along with the conceit of their supposed preeminence. Most of those who enjoyed the slightest amount of fame barely gave me the time of day. "What is this going to do for me—to donate an hour of my life to you?" they'd say. On the last night of my travels around Texas, however, I happened to meet Terry Funk, a legend of blood-and-gore hardcore wrestling now well into his fifties. He was standing in the parking lot of a Denny's, sucking on a toothpick, enjoying the soft night air before getting on the road home to Amarillo. I told him what I was doing, and about the frustrations I was having. He laughed, not surprised. Then he sucked on his toothpick some more, and I tried to think of a question that would unlock the mysteries of professional wrestling.

Funk doesn't mind seeming like a punch-drunk coot, but he is widely acknowledged as one of the good guys in the business, as well as one of the wisest, and he must have known what I was angling for.

"It's all about the fans, brother," he said and left it at that.

AND WHERE fans gathered, I quickly learned, was where everybody else congregated these days: the Internet.

If you watched the nightly news at the turn of the century, you would think that Americans mostly cared about the economy, politics, sports, show business, science, technology, their health, the weather. . . . But you'd be wrong. What they cared about, according to the domain requests tabulated by Google, the world's most popular search engine, was professional wrestling. Indeed, wrestling was among the most searched subjects on the Internet, right up there with sex and God, and every bit as mystifying.

In short order, I happened upon the Web page of Mr. Slick, who, despite his name, was not a wrestler. He was a fan. But not just any fan, he told me in an email. He was "the most unique wrestling fan in the country." I'd understand, he said, if I joined him and a bunch of other fans on an overnight trip by chartered bus, first to Bethlehem, Pennsylvania, and then on to Philadelphia, for two shows staged by the hardcore company Extreme Championship Wrestling.

Seven years earlier, when *Sports Illustrated* declared wrestling all but dead, ECW was just another struggling independent promotion of unknown, untrained, and often unpaid players, staging wrestling's version of community theater in parking lots and legion halls around the Northeast. From performing in front of fifty fans on a good night in 1995, ECW was now broadcast nationally, Friday nights on cable television, and a million households were tuning in. That was only a tiny share of the forty million American viewers who watched the thirty hours of wrestling broadcast each week. World Wrestling Entertainment had most of that audience, broadcasting from at least two different towns, week after week, without break, year after year. The McMahons liked to say they staged the last family-hour variety show on television, appealing to adults who (according to the company's market research analysts) make more money, are more professional, better educated, and more involved with their families than the average American. "This is America plus—a slightly higher-than-average profile, sort of like the Rainbow Coalition," a company flack once told me. The spiel, complete with United Way–style testimonials to community service, wasn't entirely disingenuous. Except for the circus and Sunday church services, you were not likely to see a more heartwarming example of multigenerational togetherness than at a live WWE show.* The catch was, the majority of wrestling fans were not quite full-fledged adults. They were boys roughly between the ages of sixteen and twenty-four. And those I met in Queens, New York, waiting for their bus to Bethlehem, were its hard and dependable core.

Despite an email detailing exactly what he would be wearing that weekend, what music he would be listening to, and what wrestling magazines he would be reading, I was unable to pick out Mr. Slick among the dozens of boys waiting for their bus at the back entrance of the Queen's Center Mall. Just as his website was indistinguishable from thousands of other electronic mash notes boys kept in honor of their favorite wrestling stars, Mr. Slick turned out to be just another self-conscious seventeen-year-old wearing black jeans, a black ECW T-shirt, black Nike sneakers, carrying a change of black clothes in his black JanSport book bag. What made him so

---

*In 2002, a British court ruled that the World Wildlife Fund had prior claim to the WWF acronym. Launching a clever "Get the 'F' Out" advertising campaign, the World Wrestling Federation was renamed World Wrestling Entertainment. Although many of the events and interviews discussed here occurred before the name change, for convenience and consistency I refer to the promotion as WWE throughout.

unique, Mr. Slick explained, was how totally devoted he was to professional wrestling.

"So," I asked, "shouldn't you say that you're the most 'dedicated' wrestling fan in the country?"

"No, because what I'm saying is, there's no one else like me."

"But everyone here looks like you?"

"Right. We're all unique. That's what makes wrestling fans different. We're the same in how unique we are."

O N THE hardcore independent scene, men wrestled in barbed wire, in fire, on glass, and on thumbtacks. I expected fans would be similarly demented—the American equivalent of British football hooligans, say, attacking anything that represented civilized society. If anything, though, the interchangeably lumpy boys I met that April weekend were docile to a fault, waiting for someone, anyone, to take charge of their lives. The driving narrative of virtually every wrestler's career was his search for personal significance. But these fans seemed to take a freaked pleasure in their own insignificance. Not athletic themselves, or artistic, or attractive, or consciously rebellious, or even magnificently repellent, they were just kind of . . . ill-defined, pupating, like giant babies, still struggling to get their bodies to behave. They seemed to consider regular exercise and the basics of hygiene and grooming prissy. They were not beyond hope. Three months of basic training and they might have been whipped into shape. But their resistance to self-improvement represented a statement of profound identification, a personal avowal, like a monk's tonsure.

There were fifty-four of them on the bus (plus one guy's girlfriend and one boy's mother), and as we made our way fitfully onto the Triborough Bridge and onto the New Jersey Turnpike, they morphed in my mind into one awesomely enthusiastic young man. He was about nineteen years old and still lived at home, with his mother. His father wasn't really in the picture. A below-average student, he did not go to college but worked in a girly retail job he was ashamed of—like, behind the counter at a Mrs. Field's Cookies. Sports, the traditional vector of most teenage boys' fantasies, didn't much interest him. He didn't follow Teddy Roosevelt's doctrine of the strenuous life. He was not "the 'boys-will-be-boys' kind of boy" that the magazine *Physical Culture* hailed a century ago. He brandished signs declaring himself a nerd, a geek, a freak, a dork, a slob. "Fat, Ugly and Stupid," said one guy's T-shirt, just about summing it up. "My Life Sucks, Please Shoot Me," said a sign that a pimply boy planned on holding at tonight's show.

I, though, felt like the weirdo new kid on the school bus, beseeching every face for a possible friend. Kyle, sitting across the aisle, must have seen the anxious look on my face. A half hour into the trip, he leaned over and told me not to worry. "You're not going to find stupider people in the world than at a wrestling show," he said, sotto voce.

"Ninety percent of them just look fucking weird," his friend Tom added.

"They're like Trekkies, but worse," Kyle went on. "They're fucking ridiculous. They're semiretarded; it embarrasses you. I go to these wrestling shows and look at these guys, and I think, 'Do I look like them?' "

Well, yes, he did. But gathered together on a chartered bus, none of these boys seemed to feel like the "pale, narrow-chested, hunched-up, miserable specimens" that Robert Baden-Powell, founder of the Boy Scouts, said would come of young men who sat around watching others play games. Nor did they seem the sort of angry, alienated, depressed, and self-destructive boys who, according to a Harvard University study on the culture of manhood, were being poisoned by "toxic" masculine ideals. "The boys in Littleton are the tip of the iceberg," declared William Pollack, author of *Real Boys: Rescuing Our Sons from the Myths of Boyhood,* "and the iceberg is all boys." Yet between those in the back drinking malt liquor out of forty-ounce bottles and those in front arguing about whether wearing a bright and brassy championship replica belt was or was not totally gay, none of the boys on this bus seemed "out of control and out of touch."

Actually, some of these boys were not boys at all. Many were legal adults. Some were married. Some had children. But none were ready to put childish things aside. "My wife, she's pretty immature," one guy volunteered, seeing as I was taking notes. "She got mad and what she did is, she took it out on my action figures."

"*Bitch!*"

"It's been tough. Me and my brother, we get together and set 'em up in a ring and pose them in all the moves."

"*Fuckin'-A!*"

"To be fair, she didn't destroy 'em all. Some I broke myself."

They knew what people said—that wrestling was moronic and absurd, sexist and violent—but they also knew that its critics hadn't experienced firsthand the fun of misbehaving, of letting all their private and individual worries get absorbed and expiated in a crowd's triumphant foolishness.

Tooling down the New Jersey Turnpike, they wanted to make one more thing clear to me: they were not total idiots. They knew that everything in wrestling, from the entrances to the finishing moves, was scripted. Scripted but not, they insisted, fake, because fake implied that there was nothing true and transporting about their experience, and that just wasn't the case. Most of the time they watched slack-jawed in the sincere belief that the wrestlers, who seemed to lead such prodigal lives, were mythic heroes come to life. When Stone Cold Steve Austin drank beer and gave his boss the finger, they saw a rugged individualist who listened to no man but himself— not a loyal company man doing exactly as told. When they beheld Dwayne Johnson, a.k.a. The Rock, they saw the very paragon of he-man masculinity—not a failed football player who primped and preened his well-waxed body like a drag queen. On the other hand, they talked astutely about demographics, Nielsen ratings, and buy rates. They compared the relative effectiveness of different marketing strategies. Kibitzing about wrestlers was a way into headier discussions about wrestling's "existential themes," as Kyle across the aisle put it. That was the main appeal of wrestling, he said—how a wrestler's true personality was revealed through his character. "Everyone who doesn't watch wrestling will say the same thing, that it's fake," he said. "But my response is that, on a certain level, everything is phony. What makes a good performance is when a wrestler is working right on the edge, so close to the edge that he has gone over to the real."

Christopher, sitting in front of us, was not so sure about

that. "Come on! That's just crap," he said, craning his neck around. "This is just brutality at its most basic, just two guys knocking each other around. That's its appeal. You don't have to be a genius to do it."

Kyle loftily did not respond.

"The wrestlers who get the pop nowadays," he continued serenely, "who get over with the fans, are the ones who are letting their true personalities shine through."

"I hate to make the analogy to homosexuality . . ." his friend Tom began.

"It's kind of hard not to make," an older guy, the one who had come with his girlfriend, who *had* a girlfriend, put in.

"But," Tom continued, "it's like everyone is coming out of the closet, just being themselves."

Kyle agreed: "It's the whole inner-beauty thing."

By now, it had gotten dark outside. The bus hummed along soothingly, free of traffic. A video compilation of famously gruesome matches played on the monitors running down the bus's aisle, like a lullaby, putting the boys sitting behind me in a pleasant dreamlike trance. Up where I was sitting, the spectacle of Terry Funk and Sabu becoming hopelessly entangled in barbed wire reminded Kyle and Tom and Christopher of all the wrestlers who had come to sorry ends. They began listing dozens who had died of unnatural causes in recent years—a roll call that, far from unnerving them, seemed to invest wrestling with extra meaning. Wrestlers suffered and sacrificed, some even died "for the love of the fans," they said.

"We, the true wrestling fans, know that deep down in their hearts, even when they act like assholes, they love us," Urial Yakobov, the seventeen-year-old boy who had organized the trip, said. "That's why they do it."

"But how can you tell they love you?" I asked.

"That! Right there!" he said.

Everyone gaped at the video monitors. Now it was Mick Foley we were watching, a wrestler these fans had known coming up in ECW working under the nom de mats Dude Love and Cactus Jack, who had more recently become famous as Mankind, a WWE star and the author of *two* bestselling memoirs. This mutilated, multitalented personage was picking himself up from a twenty-foot fall from a chain-link cage, and there was something very wrong with his face.

I asked: "What's that white thing sticking out of his nose?"

"Dude, that's his tooth!" several boys said all at once.

"What the . . . ?" I started to say.

"You just have to experience it to understand," Urial said. "It has to be in your heart. You have to believe in it. There's no other way to explain it."

SAW MEN CRYING that weekend in Pennsylvania. I saw men in bikini briefs and spandex tights, men hugging, holding hands, fondling, and cradling one another, men hung upside down on the corner ropes, in what the ringside announcers called "the Tree of Woe." I also saw men in camouflage battle fatigues, acting conspicuously like men, hitting each other with metal folding chairs, with beer cans, with fluorescent lights, with hammers; men crashing through particleboard tables; men pounding their chests like Tarzan.

Professional wrestling is pure ritual, and the basic format is as predictable as a Road Runner cartoon: about ten matches, some one-on-one affairs, others two- or three-man tag-team routines, all of them lasting about fifteen minutes, counting the hullabaloo of the wrestlers' entrances and exits. Yes, there are "I quit" matches, battles royal, bunkhouse brawls, and something called a three-way. There is midget wrestling and lady wrestling and coed wrestling. There are ladder matches, thumbtack matches, cage matches, glass matches, barbed-wire matches, brass-knux matches, first-blood matches, hair-versus-hair matches, lumberjack matches, dog-collar matches, bull-rope matches, scaffold matches, strap matches, and exploding death matches. There are old-school wrestlers, submission wrestlers, hardcore wrestlers, hillbilly wrestlers, masked Mexican lucha libre wrestlers, shoot wrestlers, and wrestlers who just talk a lot and never actually wrestle. There are babyfaces (good guys), heels (bad guys), 'tweeners, and crossovers. Wrestlers specialize in acrobatics, in incurring pain, in bleeding, in being ugly, in being fat, in being hairy, in being Canadian or Russian or German or Middle Eastern or Asian. Wrestlers act rich and snooty, poor and stupid. They act tough and prissy, straight and gay. Some are known for their finishing moves—leg drops, fist drops, atomic drops, elbow drops, drop kicks, and tomahawk chops. Others are famous for chokeholds, claw holds, sleeper holds, testicular holds, and step-over toeholds. You have arm breakers, arm draggers, airplane spinners, back rakers, back breakers, boot scrapers, flap jackers, and gator busters. I have seen wrestlers use branding irons, two-by-fours, forks, fishing hooks, baseball bats, guitars, cowbells, canes, crutches, crowbars, wheelchairs, weed whackers, tennis racquets, golf clubs, cell phones, polo mallets, pizza cutters, soap, salt, and all variety of household utensils. I've seen the same wrestler wearing both jodhpurs and diapers.

For all that apparent variety, however, the structure of a

wrestling show, from the grand entrances to the required finishing moves, has remained virtually unchanged for nearly a century. Whether we're talking about Vince McMahon's publicly traded $1 billion WWE or Adrian "The Polish Pitbull" Eiderowicz's backyard federation in Maspeth, Long Island, wrestling has always been a spectacle of highly dramatic, strangely costumed people desperate to be noticed. They make their fabulously bombastic entrances one or two or three at a time, soliciting the crowd's praise or censure. Sometimes, a manager or a female "valet" accompanies them. Sometimes, there will be what is called a "run-in" of a wrestler's trusty associates, throwing the match into chaos. Sometimes, if the script dictates, an inspector from the state athletic commission will step in and end the match with a disqualification. And sometimes—although this is rare—after the wrestlers have exhausted themselves in the heat of passion, they will agree to disagree. Basically, though, what almost every match boils down to is a status contest of domination and submission. Unlike a boxing match, it is not a real athletic contest; it is a theatrical enactment of one.

WWE and WCW gussied up the ritual with a lot of shock-and-awe pyrotechnics and the most innovative use of video graphics this side of MTV. Not so Extreme Championship Wrestling. "This isn't some corporate bullshit," said Tod Gordon, the owner of a Philadelphia pawnshop who started ECW in 1993, throwing monthly ragtag shows in a local bar, and who still kept a hand in the operation after selling the promotion to his booker, Paul Heyman, a.k.a. Paul E. Dangerously. "This is blood and guts, tits and ass, plain and simple. We're about guys crashing through three tables onto a concrete floor. We're about saying 'motherfucker' on TV. We're the guys who can't get jobs, guys who are drug addicts, guys getting out of jail. We're the Little Engine That Could . . . WWE and WCW, they have billions of dollars. We not only have no money, we're constantly in debt. But we've taken off because we deliver what we promise, without marketing and merchandizing and pyrotechnics and all that other bullshit."

Indeed, a visitor from the Middle Ages would not have felt out of place at an ECW show in Viking Hall, located in a warehouse directly beneath Interstate 95, in an industrial section of South Philadelphia. The bleachers surrounding the simple stage (the ring) would not have been made of aluminum; the performers would not have had microphones amplifying their soliloquies; and the dingy hall would have been lit by flickering fire instead of the sickly green tint of humming fluorescent lights. But performing their blissfully puerile skits in colorfully homemade costumes before a festive and forgiving audience, the wrestlers (with their medieval ideas of personal hygiene and grooming) might well have been the clueless mechanicals in *A Midsummer Night's Dream*.

Urial Yakobov's weekend bus package assured us of our own section in the stands. Yet we arrived two hours early anyway, getting in a line that snaked a quarter-mile through the pilings of the thumping overpass. The boys at the front—and it was almost entirely teenage boys—had been there since early that morning, talking wrestling and talking trash. They would make fun of one another's weight, height, race, of the clothes they wore, of their mothers, of their latent homosexuality, of their being from this or that town—and then they'd high-five each other, no hard feelings. Those of us on the bus had the advantage of coming as a group, and as far as we were concerned, everyone else in line was a homo, except for the

few girls, who were whores. It had a unifying effect, this slanging. An intoxicating sense of esprit de corps spread up and down the line, prompting spontaneous cheers of solidarity.

By now I was beginning to see that Urial Yakobov was more than the organizer of the bus trip. At least until the show started, he was the de facto leader of the entire congregation. Physically, he was not in any better shape than the other boys. His teeth were a mess. He hadn't grown into his nose. But someone had given the dorky, insecure boys permission to openly enjoy wrestling. It was the cool people who did this, and Urial was cool. He didn't know it. He didn't think about it. But boys like Mr. Slick took their cues from him. And so did I, dazzled by his zeal. "Wrestling is politically incorrect," Urial had told me on the bus. "That's what's so cool about it, because in real life I would never say the things that I say at a wrestling show. My attitude is that everybody is human, just the same as you and me. But at a show, I'm going to yell, 'Take it up the ass, faggot!' and cheer when my favorite wrestler beats the shit out of the guy. Because if you're a fan, that's your role. When we curse at someone and call him names, we want him to curse back at us, to call us faggots and pussies and shit like that. That's what makes it so fun. It's part of the show."

Born in Uzbekistan of Jewish parents, Urial had come to New York at age eleven by way of Moscow and Tel Aviv and had struggled to fit in, until one fateful Friday night a couple of years after he arrived. He had been playing basketball at a community center near his apartment in Queens when a wrestling road crew showed up to load in for a show that night. Urial didn't want to leave the court, but the crew offered to let him see the show for free if he did. He wasn't a fan; in fact, he claimed to despise wrestling. But for some reason he stayed to watch.

It would be an epiphany, a life-changing event.

"These guys, they took these chairs and just beat the shit out of these other guys," he recalled. "You had women beating the shit out of each other. And I was like, 'How cool is that!' I was smiling, I was cursing, I was cheering. I just got a good feeling inside. And from that day on, I knew—this makes me happy!"

Now, filing into the hall, Urial had the astonished, ecstatic look of a Holy Roller at a tent revival.

"We're on TV!" he began as soon as we found our seats. It was one of two basic chants—the four-stress chant (which also worked for "She's Got Herpes!" or "You're a Homo!"), and the three-stress chant (for "You Fucked Up!" or "We Want Chairs!"). The boys would chant, clap three or four times, depending on the syllabication, chant, clap. . . . Then, as if cued, they would all chant something else—usually in response to whatever caught Urial's eye.

After exulting that they were seated in direct line with the television cameras, Urial suddenly noticed a nice-looking girl.

"Show Your Tits! Show Your Tits!" he chanted, and was instantly joined by every other boy in the arena, including the girl's boyfriend.

When the girl obliged, the boys instantly erupted in another triumphant chant, with similar meter and phrasing: "You Dumb Bitch! You Dumb Bitch!"

For another girl who refused their attentions, they had another: "You Fat Cunt! You Fat Cunt!"

Vile as this must seem, the tenor of the epithets did not actually sound hateful or even degrading. The fun was all in the exorbitant use of language. And if it made any difference, the boys mainly ridiculed one another—as when, for instance, an enormously fat fan named Glen with ringside seats turned around to those of us in the bleachers, dropped his pants, and pulled his butt cheeks apart for a clear and entirely too memorable view of his anus.

"Homo! Suck my dick!" they screamed in ecstasies of delight, as Glen daintily held up his dresslike football jersey and, pants around his ankles, performed a mincing little dance.

"We want male porn!" a kid sitting near me screamed out at its conclusion.

Finally, the show began with a poetry reading from announcer Joel Gertner ("I have a whim for some trim . . ."), followed by discussion about whether Raven had taken a bounty out on Tommy Dreamer. Mr. Raven denied the allegations, and although he was not to be trusted (having once brainwashed another wrestler's son), in one of the early matches of the evening he came to Mr. Dreamer's rescue, before Mike Awesome clotheslined both men. (Why would Mr. Awesome do this? "Because," he explained, "I'm awesome!") Messrs. Rhino, Tajiri, and Sandman—each making an entrance amid a cloud of smoke and strobe lights—snorted, spewed green mist, and smashed beer cans against their foreheads. Super Crazy clocked Little Guido with a crowbar. Jack Victory clocked Mr. Super Crazy with a cowbell. Big Sal clocked Mr. Victory with a ring bell. New Jack hit lots of people with a crutch, then staple-gunned dollar bills to their cheeks. Dusty Rhodes took out one man after another with his bionic elbow. Lance Storm sat on Nova's face. Balls Mahoney took Justin Credible's hand and rubbed it over his own genitals. Mr. Credible retaliated by placing the ring bell over Mr. Mahoney's crotch and striking it with a hammer. A couple of valets with pneumatic breasts called each other skanks. The men bounced back and forth off the ring ropes, kicked each other in the crotch, disregarded the referee, and everybody took turns getting thrown through particleboard tables. Several wrestlers said that it would be a "privilege" to kick another wrestler's ass, and proceeded to do just that. Raven and Tommy Dreamer hugged, however, and, with Tommy's ascension to World Champion, let bygones be bygones. Unfortunately, in all defiance of good sportsmanship, Justin Credible spoiled the bonhomie, appearing out of nowhere to steal the championship belt before Mr. Dreamer could ever wear it.

Fans had a long and seemingly intimate history with each of these performers. Even before a wrestler made his pompous appearance, it took the playing of but one note of his theme music to elicit an instantaneous reaction from every boy in the arena. But if absence is the highest form of presence, the biggest star of the show was someone the fans never saw that night, the wizard of their Oz, Paul Heyman, working behind the scenes. The son of an Auschwitz survivor, Heyman understood that this blend of sentimentality and barbarism had a potent effect on the hearts and minds of teenage boys. Urial regarded Heyman as "a true genius." Even grown-up men genuflected to him, calling him God. His influence was indeed ubiquitous, with WWE and WCW doing their best to cop ECW's ideas, talent, and its unruly attitude. By rejecting the dubious idea that wrestling should be family entertainment, he had rewritten the wrestling rules, fans claimed, pitting heel against heel, babyface against babyface.

Still, what made the show so intensely satisfying was not that you never knew what was going to happen next, as the boys kept telling me. But that you did.

"Okay, you're right—it's predictable, what's going to happen," Urial admitted afterward. "It's totally obvious. But to me, when they're beating the shit out of each other, the truth is, I don't care if it sucks. As long as I can scream my head off, yelling shit, throwing shit, calling girls sluts, calling other guys faggots, I'm totally happy."

To my surprise, so was I.

# CHAPTER TWO

THE FARTHER ONE GETS FROM FOLLY, THE LESS
AND LESS HE LIVES.          —ERASMUS

ISTORIES OF professional wrestling typically begin in ancient and biblical times. You'll read about Jacob wrestling an angel, the holds and falls depicted on the walls of Egyptian temples, and the mighty Milo of Greece, who could kill an ox with his bare hands. The historians then skip ahead a couple thousand years, to King Henry VIII, George Washington, and Abraham Lincoln, all of whom wrestled, and to John Milton, who did not but thought highly of the sport just the same. "Wrestling, in a noble, manly forbearing and human practice

of it," he writes, "is the indigenous offspring of steady courage and love of gymnastic exercise."

I am only guessing, but the author of *Paradise Lost* probably would not have been a fan of the professional wrestling we know today. He would, however, have been familiar with its theatrical traditions. From pagan times up through the first decades of the twentieth century, theater was something much closer in style and substance to professional wrestling than today's self-involved drama, in which audiences sit in rows and actors talk as if they were alone and entirely real. The Greek term for conflict is *agon* (as in agony and anguish, struggle and violence), and the staging of ritual combat between forces of light and dark, virtue and villainy, has been the basis of virtually every theatrical tradition around the world. Medieval miracle, mystery, and morality plays featured saints dueling dragons, angels duking it out with devils, and personified virtues wrestling with vices. Staged for a largely illiterate audience, the productions were grandiloquent and spectacular. They were also directly relevant to concerns of the times—a tradition kept alive in the days of the rabble-rousing French Revolution, when street performers used slapstick comedy for political effect.

Pro wrestlers haven't consciously tried to keep ancient theatrical traditions alive, but from the very beginning the contests were much more than sport. The business started with catch-as-catch-can, collar-and-elbow wrestling, the brute strength of its champions creating a semblance of credibility. The first truly "professional" American wrestler was Civil War veteran William Muldoon, who discovered that he could make more money brawling in Bowery bars than as a New York City policeman. The "Cumberland" style of the day, in which opponents stood chest to chest, resting their chins on each other's shoulders until one man was thrown off his feet, produced some epic battles. In 1880, "The Solid Man," as Muldoon was known, went nine and a half hours with William Miller, before bartenders doused the gaslights at four in the morning. In truth, the barkeeps were probably bored. Even at the time, though, there was something not quite cricket about the sport. The late honorable secretary to the Wrestling Society of London was already troubled by the "equivocal conduct" of professional wrestlers, calling ground wrestling "a kind of dogfight utterly opposed to our notions of sport." Perhaps the most legendary hustler was Fred Grubmier, a six-foot-six, 180-pound galoot who wandered around the Midwest pretending to be retarded, only to walk away with thousands of dollars in side bets after beating the barnstorming champions of the day. Another wrestler who passed himself off as a Native American, Chief Chewacki, was really a Serbian gypsy who trained monkeys to burglarize homes. Muldoon was exempt from disdain, however. Wrestling historian Nat Fleischer averred that he was "truly handsome, kind and scholarly." And to the novelist Theodore Dreiser, who recuperated from a nervous breakdown at the champion's sanitarium in upstate New York, the "shapely and grand" Muldoon was one of the most remarkable men he had ever met—"very princely in build and manner."

As melodrama, wrestling has always depended on the fiction of superior virtue. Frank Gotch, the next star to come along in the early years of the twentieth century, was famous for eye-gouging, hair-pulling, and slathering his body in kerosene and coconut oil. Instead of shaking hands at the beginning of a championship match, as was the custom, he'd dive for his opponents' legs, pinning them in seconds. Yet being an Iowa farm boy, he was considered the beau ideal of

American grit. To Chicago sportswriter Ed Smith, Gotch "typified exactly what an artist would seek to portray on his canvas in bringing into one figure the composite virility of America." His European adversary was cut from different cloth. Born in Russia of German ancestry, the debonair George Hackenschmidt spoke several languages, a skill that came in handy touring the music halls of Europe. Later, he would become physical education instructor to the British House of Lords. To such things "Gotch turned a scornful face," Smith said, being "natively suspicious of all things citified."

Thus the Gotch–Hackenschmidt rivalry was framed as a contest between homely American manliness and effete European dandyism. The men met twice. Hackenschmidt was the two-to-one favorite in their 1908 match at Dexter Park, near the Chicago stockyards. But unable to get any kind of grip on the oiled-up Gotch (it was "like trying to grip a well-buttered eel," he complained), Hackenschmidt quit the match when the referee refused to intervene. The carping that followed set the stage for one of the most energetically promoted sporting events ever—and one of the most controversial. Students of wrestling history obsess about what went down in 1911 when the two met for a rematch before a crowd of thirty-five thousand fans, once again in Chicago. That Gotch won is not disputed. The question is whether he won fair and square. A few weeks before the bout, Hackenschmidt told reporters that he had "achieved that perfect poise and balance of all my qualities and attributes which is known only to the athlete in perfect trim." But days before the fight, he was supposedly injured in training. Some say The Russian Lion chickened out, faking the injury; others that Gotch sent one of his goons to break Hack's legs, à la figure skater Tonya Harding and her ex-husband Jeff

Gillooly. Agnostics say both men colluded in "the greatest fiasco ever perpetrated upon the American public"—that rather than give up the big payday, Hackenschmidt limped into the ring, assured that Gotch would carry him through a reasonably satisfying show. That was not the way it worked out, though. The "Thunderbolt from Humboldt" quickly threw Hackenschmidt in two straight falls. Outraged fans, realizing they'd been had (if not sure by whom), all but destroyed Comiskey Park.

ALTHOUGH MAT WRESTLING soon fell into disrepute, the 1911 fight marked the beginning of a far more interesting era of intrigue. The fight's promoter was Jack Curley, who also managed the speaking tours of William Jennings Bryan and the American concert dates of the Vatican choir. Relocating to New York after the debacle in Chicago, Curley soon had three of the better-known wrestlers working for him, pretending to compete against one another for the heavyweight title. He also began collaborating with two of the more enterprising hucksters of the day, Jack Pfefer and Toots Mondt. By then they had all come to the realization that an old-style Greco-Roman wrestling match "is not an inspiring spectacle," as the journalist A. J. Liebling put it, "except to Greco-Roman wrestlers." Though sticking with the pretense of legitimate athleticism, matches now became exhibitions of acrobatics, melodramatic plot reversals, and vaudevillian finishes. Whether they admitted it or not, most fans understood the titles meant nothing, and that the humbug was at least half the fun.

Certainly the chicanery appealed to some creative and resourceful men. When Curley was not promoting wrestling, he was hustling the talents of opera singers. His associate, Ray

Fabiani, a concert violinist, would promote an Antonio Rocco–Johnny Valentine match that had been set to a Handel opera. Houston promoter Paul Boesch, a decorated soldier in World War I, who was active in pro wrestling in the 1930s and 1940s, wrote a book of poetry about clouds and angels and happiness. He also came up with the concept of tag teams. Others had the inspiration for ice-cream matches, feather-and-molasses matches, lard matches, tomato-and-blueberry matches. A promoter in Wisconsin filled the ring with fish. Another in San Francisco marketed his shows specifically to the Bay Area's Filipino population—on the theory that, as they were small people, he could cram more of them in an arena.

In the early 1930s, the syndicate of Curley, Mondt, Pfefer, and Fabiani, joined by Billy Sandow and Paul Bowser, effectively consolidated the business in the Northeast, laying the foundation for World Wrestling Entertainment's base of operations today. They created the basic structure of a wrestling show, coined much of its lexicon, and devised many of the ways a match could end, like having wrestlers bump heads and knock each other unconscious. They were wily businessmen, adept at capitalizing on a wrestler's extracurricular interests. Wrestling doctors, dentists, and decorators barnstormed the country. Each week they and the bookers who produced the road shows received telegrammed instructions from the trust with "results" written in code. Wrestlers who refused orders didn't work. It was as simple as that—until Jim Londos came along later in the decade.

Londos was the first wrestler—one of the first athletes or actors, for that matter—to realize that his fame, regardless of its merits, carried more clout than even the promoters had. Born Christopher Theophelus in Argos, Greece, he had come to San Francisco as a teenage cabin boy. Taking construction jobs on the side, Londos found work in a vaudeville tumbling act. He also posed nude for figure-drawing classes. In the ring, he adopted a proletarian shtick, wearing construction clothes and calling himself The Wrestling Plasterer. His favorite writer, Jack London, inspired the name Londos. How "The Little Giant" rode that name to outsized fame seemed wholly inexplicable to old wrestling hands. Unlike the champions who preceded him, Londos couldn't really wrestle. That had always seemed important—"fellows who could hold their own by fair means or foul, when called upon to do so," as Mondt put it. Certainly nobody figured Londos could fill Madison Square Garden. Yet fourteen thousand New Yorkers paid to see him throw Gino Garibaldi in forty-six minutes. Six weeks later, twice as many came to see him again. For Londos's next New York date, Curley had to book Yankee Stadium.

In lieu of a champion who could really wrestle, Curley wanted one "who we know we can exploit properly." The syndicate believed it had such a man in Londos. Curley also thought people came to at least see a credible facsimile of wrestling. But Londos, with his wavy black hair and dazzling white teeth, had something else to offer, something the country was just becoming familiar with. He had celebrity. He had star power. "What a man! What an artist!" *The New Yorker* raved, only somewhat ironically. The old guard was nonplussed. The boy didn't know his place . . . winning had gone to his head . . . why, he didn't think he should lose. . . . But, then, why should Londos lose? As to actual wrestling ability, the titles had not meant anything for decades. Getting over— that is, creating the aura of celebrity—was all that counted now. And nobody in two decades had been more "over" than

Londos. "I'm the big drawing card," he said, demanding more than one-third of the gate and a guarantee of fifty thousand dollars if he lost an unplanned "shoot"—a real, unscripted fight. When the trust still insisted he drop the belt to Dick Shikat, he sent a succinct wire from Chicago: "I'm through and what are you going to do about it?"

It is the classic wrestling story. Just when everyone had figured out how to work together to make some serious money (during the Great Depression, no less), egos got in the way. After Londos dissed the trust, the man who had always done its dirty work, Jack Pfefer, also found himself on the outs. Pfefer was a diminutive Polish Jew who had come to the country as a stagehand with a Moscow ballet company. The things people said of him (that he was dirty and devious, a corvine nosepicker with terrible breath) smacked of rank anti-Semitism. Wrestling made for even stranger bedfellows than politics, however, and in desperation Pfefer turned to Shikat, a German eager to return to the fatherland and join the Nazis. Stiffed yet again, Pfefer finally took revenge on the whole racket. "Them thiefs is stealin'," he told the *New York Daily Mirror*. "It's all a carnival with a bunch of fakers and the public is not to take it serious."

W HEN A FLOOD of exposés immediately began appearing in magazines and newspapers, it was not the wrestlers and promoters who felt exposed, it was the fans—as credulous chumps. Sportswriters in the pay of the promoters could also no longer peddle the fiction of wrestling's legitimacy. Ever the loyal enthusiast, even Nat

Fleischer had to acknowledge that "the titular bouts of the past were far more interesting from the point of view of competition."

It took more than a decade for everyone to realize that the chicanery of the present would prove to be more interesting as cultural theater. Nobody threw in the towel exactly, but attendance plummeted and the trust broke apart. "It was a period of re-evaluation," Liebling wrote. Each promoter had his own regional territory now: Bowser in Boston, Fabiani in Philadelphia, Mondt in Los Angeles, and the five-foot-one, 110-pound Pfefer bouncing around the country, from New York to Toledo to Nashville, surviving with ladies and midgets. ("I am very proud of some of my monstrosities," he said. "I treat them like a mother who beats up her baby.") Wrestling retreated to the small towns and ethnic neighborhoods, and if not for television and a blue-eyed, blond-haired high school dropout named George Raymond Wagner probably would have remained there.

Wagner was a tenant farmer's son, a big blond bruiser who nevertheless loved preening and primping and practical jokes. He called his pranks "swerves," a term that wrestlers still use today. "A swerve a day," he liked to say, "keeps the blues away." After working briefly in the Houston shipyards, he made his wrestling debut playing it straight, as it were, calling himself Elmer Schmitt, and, like a lot of wrestlers, wondered what he was doing wrong. "Many a time I lay in bed in my cheap hotel, hungry and broke," he later recalled. Only after meeting and soon marrying (in the ring) a cashier at a movie theater in Eugene, Oregon, did Wagner start playing the femme soon known to all of America as Gorgeous George.

"This little gal, she came to every match he was in," the promoter Don Owen, whose broadcasts from Portland I had grown up watching on desultory Saturday afternoons, told me on a drizzly December evening shortly before he died in 2002. "George had her sit in the first row, and she'd holler something awful. She was a good seamstress and started making him some fancy silk robes. One night she presented a blue sequined robe to him in the ring, and since she made it—he wasn't acting like a sissy yet—he took extra care folding it up instead of tossing it aside like most guys did. I was getting a hell of a lot of tree fellers and log haulers coming to the shows in those days, and they'd all have ringside seats. Well, the more time George took, the more they booed him. And his wife—she was a little fireball—she'd say, 'Keep your big mouth shut!' Finally, one night she just turned around and slapped one of the loggers in the face. That did it. George jumped over the ropes and knocked 'em through all the ringside seats. When he got back in the ring, everybody in the goddamn place booed the hell out of him. And from then on, no matter what he did, they booed him. He didn't give a damn and I didn't give a damn, either, so long as we made money. And we did. He got to be quite an attraction. They'd drive two hundred miles to see him. See, they didn't have any basketball or football on TV back then; all they had was me, and I was making money hand over fist."

Soon Wagner began entering an arena to "Pomp and Circumstance," wearing a silver lamé robe, while his "manservant" Geoffrey dutifully perfumed the ring. He would primp his luxurious locks, toss golden bobby pins to the crowd, and tell women they were disgusting. Dining out, he'd have Geoffrey spray the other diners with a disinfectant he called Chanel No. 10. At a charity event, he danced the Viennese waltz with Burt Lancaster. For comics like Bob Hope, Wagner was sure-fire material, the way Michael Jackson or Anna Nicole Smith is today. This was 1949, though, a year Wagner sold out the

Olympic Auditorium in Los Angeles thirty-seven times. He also headlined the first wrestling exhibition at Madison Square Garden since 1938, an event covered by the drama and movie critics of every New York newspaper. Very few performers or athletes came close to making the kind of money he did. And he kept all of it in cash, in a safe-deposit box. That way, whenever he felt like it, he could spill it all over the bank-vault floor and walk around in it, barefoot.

It's hard to imagine a happier man—or a happier time to be a professional wrestler. "It was a loony business, filled with loony people," the great Lou Thesz said of the Gorgeous George era. "We were free and independent, accountable to no one but ourselves. . . . It was a loose-as-goose life, and I loved it."

I have heard an excellent theory that the wrestling business thrives during periods of cultural anxiety. Only it is not quite true. Except for its run during the Depression, wrestling's popularity has peaked in periods of peace and prosperity. After World War II, the country was living large, and wrestling was a manifestation of that exuberance, like tail fins on the tanks we were driving. In little more than a decade, national production doubled, personal income tripled, and the middle class quadrupled. Americans were bigger and healthier and younger—nearly three inches taller, and living nearly twenty years longer than just half a century earlier—while constantly coming up with new things to buy and novel ways of amusing themselves.

Television became the primary medium through which the country processed these dizzying changes. After the war, a manufacturer of cathode-ray tubes named Allen B. DuMont attempted to develop programming for his own network, and wrestling proved a perfect fit. Even with poor reception, the broad sight gags were perfectly intelligible to viewers. And the network didn't have to produce shows from scratch. DuMont merely had to transmit from a neighborhood arena and the drama would take care of itself, as it always had. The only ingredient the network needed to add was an on-air announcer with a gift for improvisation. Knowing nothing about wrestling, DuMont's Dennis James checked out six books from the New York Public Library to skim on the taxi ride to his first broadcast from the Jamaica Arena, in Queens. He also picked up a fried chicken, which he used for sound effects. Whenever a wrestler seemed in the grip of a painful hold, he would crack a bone in the microphone.

For seven years, pro wrestling would be a prime-time staple, on all four networks. It may never have had anything like Milton Berle's audience (94.7 percent of viewers in 1948), and after DuMont went out of business, it would be relegated to local stations. Yet wrestling would be the only programming of TV's infancy to survive, kicking and screaming, into the twenty-first century.

LIKE MOST WRESTLERS, Gorgeous George had a harder time of it. Living hard and drinking heavily until the end, he would die broke, at age forty-eight, of cirrhosis of the liver, twice divorced, his stripper girlfriend having to take up a collection to pay for his burial. To his dying day, though, still wearing his silk robe, still preening even though the public had lost interest in wrestling, Wagner kept faith in Gorgeous George.

"If personality is an unbroken series of successful gestures," F. Scott Fitzgerald wrote of another American dreamer, "then there was something gorgeous about him, some heightened sensitivity to the promises of life." From The Solid Man to The Rock, wrestlers have brought those promises marvelously to life, giving body to a distinctly American ideology of achievement. William Muldoon had stood for brute strength of character, of success achieved by dint of determination and discipline. Thirty years later, with Frank Gotch, Americans were given to understand that even if they lacked European sophistication they were nobody's fool. In Londos, the country saw that success had nothing to do with talent or determination, or even cunning, and everything to do with publicity and posturing.

Probably none of these men gave much thought to what they represented. That's not how popular culture operates. Meaning does not emerge by conscious intent. It surfaces when people find something, or someone, relevant to their needs. And one thing America has always needed, clearly, are fortifying images of masculinity. Buffalo Bill, John L. Sullivan, Teddy Roosevelt, Babe Ruth, Humphrey Bogart, John Wayne, Sylvester Stallone, Arnold Schwarzenegger—it is perhaps no great mystery why the country would need these masculine figures. In the twentieth century, a lot of men began to feel like ninety-pound weaklings. Everywhere they turned, it seemed that someone was kicking sand in their face, from rapacious capitalists at the beginning of the century to fed-up feminists at the end. As the manly work of exploring the frontier and taming a wilderness neared completion, newspaper advertisements promised to "cure weak men suffering from Lost Manhood." Even those who worked in decent-paying white-collar jobs felt the loss. They had been born too late, it seemed. The days of adventure had passed them by. The only compensations seemed to come from popular culture. While scratching out a lousy living selling pencil sharpeners, Edgar Rice Burroughs wrote an adventure story for the pulps that struck a mighty chord in millions of young men longing to be lords of their own jungles. Around the same time, Harry Houdini assured audiences that his "escapism" required no magical abilities. Personal freedom was but a trick, one that any man could learn.

The professional wrestler might seem a marginal figure in America's manhood mythology; yet he has been hanging around for more than a century, endlessly reinventing himself every decade or so, forever finding new ways of remaining relevant. With Gorgeous George, the professional wrestler started saying something rather postmodern about success in the age of celebrity. He was ironic. He was playful. He was campy. He was contradictory. He turned old conventions in on themselves. He treated achievement as a glorious goof. Of celebrity he was saying what historian Daniel Boorstin would write a decade later in *The Image*: that it was essentially meaningless, just a pose. His message on manliness was much the same. And yet, in celebrating his celebrity and mocking his manhood, he went beyond a puritanical denunciation of their emptiness. He said something inspired about meaning emerging from seeming meaninglessness.

The fact that he said all these things on network television, in prime time, is remarkable. "I do not think I'm gorgeous," Wagner often said, "but what's my opinion against millions of others?" He makes an excellent point. In the supposedly conservative, conformist 1950s, millions of people who watched pro wrestling on TV did indeed believe there was something marvelous about a buxom man in drag.

Of course, that was not how the cultural custodians of the

day took Wagner's shtick. For them, professional wrestling was beneath their contempt, useful only as an illustration of our disgrace. It was what you pointed to if you needed an example of America writ ridiculous. For example, the best of the original dramatic theatrical productions of early television, Rod Serling's *Requiem for a Heavyweight*, was the story of a crucifixion, of a bruised and battered boxer reduced to the utter humiliation of pro wrestling. (Featured on TV's *Playhouse 90*, the drama swept the Emmys in 1956 and was adapted to the big screen in 1962, where it starred Jackie Gleason, Mickey Rooney, and Anthony Quinn, and included, in a cameo, a majestic young Cassius Clay.)

"Don't make me," pleads Mountain Rivera, the tragic hero, looking perfectly ludicrous in an Indian headdress. "Don't make me play a clown."

"You're not a winner anymore," his wheedling manager insists. "So when there ain't nothing left, let's make some money from the losing."

But what the film's producers were saying about them, professional wrestlers had been saying about the wider culture for decades. Success wasn't about honor or virtue; it was about doing whatever it took, no matter how dishonest or demeaning, to get attention. Bothered by that message, Serling made the classic mistake of attacking the messenger.

# CHAPTER THREE

THEY LOOK NOT ONLY FOR MORE ENTERTAIN-
MENT, BUT, AT BOTTOM, EVEN FOR MORE REAL-
ITY THAN THE REAL ITSELF CAN SHOW. . . . IT
SHOULD PRESENT ANOTHER WORLD, AND YET
ONE TO WHICH WE FEEL THE TIE.

—HERMAN MELVILLE

F ANS WERE always telling me that to really understand professional wrestling you had to believe in it. At first this seemed just another instance of the exaggerated claims that wrestling made for itself. But I soon realized that wrestling fans were quite possibly the least nihilistic people on earth, and that for them the rituals were big with meaning. Exactly *what* wrestling meant— that was a harder question to answer, but I suspected that this particular form of faith,

47

like any other, provided answers to profound longings. Not surprisingly, the small percentage of older fans, like Joe Joe Russello, Sr., the father of the eleven-year-old boy who told me I didn't know shit about wrestling, had a better perspective on what those might be.

"My wife, she thinks I'm an idiot, as far as with that. She don't believe in it," Russello said when I visited him at his home on Long Island a few weeks after we met in Philadelphia. "But my son and I, we don't miss a pay-per-view, of any federation. We go to independent shows. We buy every wrestling item. I bought out two video stores of every old tape they had. I have hundreds, if not thousands, of action figures. This is our life. We love it. It's what we believe in. Things from twenty-five years ago"—he nods to his son—"this kid can answer. Joe Joe, in 1979, Bruno Sammartino fought a legendary match in Shea Stadium against—"

"Larry Zbyszko."

"Correct. Joe Joe, the greatest tag team—"

"The Valiant Brothers, Luscious Jimmy and Handsome Johnny."

"Very good."

Clearly, these two fans knew their wrestling catechism backwards and forwards. For most of them, though, wrestling was much more than a trivial pursuit. Russello might well have become a *Sopranos*-style goomba, he said, had his childhood turned out a little differently. When he was twelve his father gave him a pistol, and it would only have been a matter of time before he, too, got involved in what he termed "family activities." But a year later, his father killed a man, and soon after was killed himself. "After that my life was tough," Russello said, "and what got me through everything was wrestling.

Believing in it. I had seen what real violence was. I was becoming violent myself, which was getting me in trouble. So I was looking for some kind of alternative that made sense to me. Also, I was a fat kid. When I was Joe Joe's age, I stood five-foot-two and weighed a hundred ninety pounds."

"That's a fat kid," I said.

"What could I do? I couldn't play basketball, I sucked in baseball. But then I got turned on to wresting. I had to watch lucha libre [masked Mexican wrestling] on the Spanish station, at eleven o'clock on Tuesday nights. And ever since, wrestling has been something that got me through tough times. My hero was Bruno Sammartino, and I was Baby Bruno. I got ridiculed for that. People looked at me like I was a dum-dum. They wanted to ruin the one thing I had going. But let me tell you—wrestling had everything I wanted. It had the glamour, it had the violence, the in-your-face attitude, the good, the bad, the weak, the meek. . . . And if you asked me right now, I can't say that it's fake."

Russello was suddenly silent.

"See," he said after a few pregnant seconds, "those words cannot come out of my mouth. I will not say them. Because saying wrestling is fake, or calling it 'sports entertainment'— that would take away the one thing I've always believed in."

MYSELF, I hadn't yet become a true believer, but after going to dozens of hardcore shows I did have an inchoate sense of what Russello's son and so many other fans kept saying I didn't understand. Joseph Campbell writes that "every last vestige of the ancient human heritage of ritual is in full decay"—except perhaps here, I thought. In the stench of beer and blood and adolescent perspiration, fans had found what a mass consumer culture no longer offered: an unmediated first-person experience. They had tapped into something vital and energizing. They were not detached connoisseurs, looking ironically down on life, concealing their anxieties in the cold comforts of satire. They were total participants in a carnival of their own making. Away from the ring, apprehensions returned. But during a show everyone could indulge his wildest fantasies, without anxiety and guilt. It was, as Gore Vidal writes, a chance to be "made free, for the time, by violence."

The violence of wrestling was not the only way young men had of trying to resolve their issues. They had violent video games, violent rap music, violent heavy metal, and the gleeful violence of *Jackass*-inspired stunts. Traditional sports redirect those aggressive impulses into a collaborative experience. Agreeing to self-imposed rules, both teammates and opponents are involved in the shared goal of having fun. In 1996, however, the National Education Association suggested that school sports may be "one of the most overlooked arenas of violence training." As an alternative, the Ms. Foundation for Women promoted role-playing, dramatizations, and games that celebrate "playing on teams for the sheer joy of playing," without keeping score or declaring winners.

Although I doubt that it was what the feminist organization had in mind, pro wrestling fit the Ms. Foundation's criteria to a T. Scores aren't kept, and nobody plays to win—the "competition" is just a fiction used to facilitate role-playing and personal expression. The dramatizations are nonetheless violent, and for good reason. Whatever else it may be, violence is never meaningless. Indeed, it communicates an excess of meaning, especially for "those who feel excluded from the modern world and who, to maintain their very status as human beings, must in some sense seek revenge," as Lewis Mumford notes.

WANTED TO try to understand, sociologically and psychologically, what gave rise to this particular expression of violence, and to consider its consequences. Clearly, you can't really understand any kind of communication unless you know who is doing the communicating—that is, who is sending the signal and who is receiving it. That gets complicated when you start talking about the semiotics of popular culture, where messages are coming at you from all directions, and everybody is both sending and receiving them. By contrast, literary communication is straightforward. One man writes a poem, say. Another man reads it. They interact only through the words on the page. That's pretty much the extent of it. The poem may be complicated, but the interaction couldn't be simpler. Still, literary theorists work themselves into a tizzy arguing about who creates the meaning of that poem. The poet? The reader? The culture? Or is meaning increate, contained in the poem itself, independent of everything else?

People make whole careers out of these sorts of arguments. Only in recent years have critics begun to see that just because art and literature lend themselves to interpretation, or provide a more congenial experience, they don't necessarily have more to say than popular culture. Humanity exists everywhere, not just on the printed page, after all. If culture is the coded exchanges of reciprocal messages, as anthropologists have defined the term, must the rhetoric of those messages be intelligible only to the few to deserve attention? If something appeals to mass tastes, is it therefore a lesser form of culture?

Are quality, originality, and imagination the only important criteria? Or is culture simply that which speaks, however crudely or elegantly, to a people's concerns? For example: we are a society consumed with measuring status. We are also obsessed with image. It may be that there are poems and plays and dance pieces that address these preoccupations, though off the top of my head I can't think of any. Even most contemporary novels seem strangely indifferent to such matters. Yet there is this one area of contemporary culture called professional wrestling that explores those concerns in every single show. In every match, actually. That isn't all wrestling deals with. It also looks at gender relations, at employee relations, at family relations, at sexuality, at power, at pain, at suffering. . . .

I should say that I'm hardly the first person to try to deconstruct professional wrestling. The brilliant French cultural critic Roland Barthes took a good crack at it fifty years ago. Wrestling, in Barthes's view, was the equal of any other kind of theater. It involved "an extended use of signs," only here they were "brought to the point of maximum obviousness."

Well, obvious or not, much of the time I was still in a complete muddle trying to make head or tail of wrestling. "Good luck!" the great NWA champion Lou Thesz told me shortly before he died a few years ago, at eighty-six. "You'll drive yourself crazy trying to figure it out." Dave Meltzer repeated the warning a few months later. For over twenty years (since he was a teenager), Meltzer has been cranking out a 26,000-word weekly newsletter, the *Wrestling News Observer*, making him perhaps the most prolific writer in America. Yet for all those millions of words, Meltzer told me he still doesn't really understand wrestling. That's why he keeps writing, hoping that someday he will.

One of the problems is pro wrestling's amorphousness. It has no season, unlike sports. It has no geographic center, unlike the fashion industry. It has no fixed "text," unlike literature. It has no meaningful chronology, unlike a news event. However, the biggest problem is that what it has to say it says in contradictions, in paradoxes that its participants (fans and wrestlers both) only half understand themselves.

That fulsome ambiguity is all in the nature of what the influential Russian literary critic Mikhail Bakhtin calls the "carnivalesque," meaning the low and bawdy culture of the "folk." In *Rabelais and His World,* Bakhtin argues that critics and historians fail to understand the true temper of a people when they ignore popular (as opposed to official and elite) culture. Writing about medieval times, he wasn't talking about maypoles and madrigal singers but, rather, something a lot like the profane participatory world of hardcore professional wrestling. "It is life itself," Bakhtin writes of the unruly festivities that were the pop culture of the day, "not a spectacle seen by the people; they live in it, and everyone participates because its very idea embraces all the people."

For a lot of people at the end of the twentieth century, young men especially, the independent wrestling scene was one of the only places where they did feel embraced. Boys were always being told they needed to learn how to express themselves. Yet it's not like they were being asked to write op-ed columns for the *New York Times* or to dilate upon the American psyche for National Public Radio. (Neither was I, for that matter.) Here, though, in a free and festive atmosphere, they were communicating their thoughts and feelings in the pithiest, most pungent way they knew how— obscenely.

"You suck dick!" a fan would yell. And if he was lucky, a wrestler would come back at him.

"If I was sucking any dick, you pussy, I'd suck . . ." the wrestler Taz started to tell a pasty-faced boy at a show I caught in Queens. Realizing what he was implying, Taz modified the imagery, but only slightly. "I'd make *you* suck *mine*! Bitch! I'd pump so much cum up your ass, you'd have to blow your nose to get it out."

Far from having his feelings hurt, the boy reveled in the attention. Others, too, had called the wrestlers homos and pussies that night, hoping that they, in return, would be called cum-guzzling faggots. But this kid hit the jackpot. It was, as Bakhtin says, "a ridicule fused with rejoicing." It was also, he adds, the stuff of human culture.

AUL HEYMAN:

"With us, the audience *is* the story. Everybody is participating. Our philosophy is: no bullshit. Our catchphrase is: 'Join the revolution.' And that's very real. Fans feel that. I feel it. When we first started, everybody was like, 'Get the fuck out of here! You're out of your fucking mind.' We weren't big enough, we weren't financed enough, we were too wild, too risqué, too dangerous, too real, too cutting-edge, too avant-garde. Yet we made it happen. We beat the system. And we did it on our own terms. The audience has been as much a part of that as anyone else. You go to WrestleMania to get your T-shirt and bobblehead doll. It's not a religious experience. ECW is. For our fans, it's not only 'I experienced it.' It's: 'I'm part of something.' It's: 'The story isn't complete without me.' Fans are providing themselves with their own good times. They're empowered. A kid speaks up and suddenly the show is about *him*! Where else does that happen? People who say it's just guys beating each other up haven't thought about what's really happening. We aren't just selling wrestling—we're selling a philosophy of life. We're saying, 'Get involved, be vocal, say what you think, say, "Fuck you," be tough, be yourself.' "

A LEXIS DE TOCQUEVILLE'S *Democracy in America* says nothing about professional wrestling *per se*. Once upon a time, though, the rambunctiousness we associate with wrestling typified American culture. The democratic rabble, expressing hostility to "refined and delicate pleasures," wanted a culture that was "fantastic, incorrect, overburdened, and loose, almost always vehement and bold," de Tocqueville noted. The eighteenth- and early-nineteenth-century theater was a raucous and at times riotous public place. Magicians, mummers, and minstrels performed on the same bill with Shakespearean actors. Butchers and mechanics could take in the soliloquies of Hamlet and the talents of a musical seal. Classically trained thespians played their parts with extravagant gusto. The actor Edwin Forrest was the Hulk Hogan of his day—an exemplar of "the muscular school, the brawny art, the biceps aesthetics"—and the audience gave as good as it got, whistling, hissing, stomping, and throwing chairs. Going to a theater was "no dainty kid-glove business," wrote an approving Walt Whitman, "but rather an electric force of muscle from full-sinewed men."

Then the culture wars began. In 1849, in fealty to Forrest, a New York audience drove the snooty English actor William

Macready from the stage in a torrent of eggs and apples. Three nights later, at the Astor Place Opera House, Macready performed *The Tragedy of Macbeth* without incident before well-heeled patrons of the arts. The real tragedy occurred outside, where more than ten thousand men of the coarser classes protested their exclusion, throwing paving stones at the theater. Armed guards opened fire, and at least twenty-two people were killed, more than 150 injured.

You might think that, as a declaration of classless democracy, the Astor Place riots would figure into a proud we're-mad-as-hell-and-aren't-going-to-take-it-anymore American mythology, first symbolized by the Boston Tea Party. The common man had risen up in the name of egalitarian ideas. This time, however, he was shot down. Though it would take time to complete the process, culture was fast becoming a sacred thing to which only cultivated people were entitled. To Henry James, the riots represented the "instinctive hostility of barbarism to culture." And from then on, the barbarians at the gates would have to look elsewhere for entertainment. Miners in Nevada wouldn't get to see Shakespeare's Desdemona playing the banjo on a billiard table anymore. The opera, where "nob and snob" had once sat side by side on plain wooden benches enjoying melodramatic plots, would soon only admit discriminating connoisseurs. By the turn of the century, concerts would require audiences to dress in styles few could afford. The price of admission was not only financial; audiences also had to make an investment of cultural capital, of education and etiquette, which few possessed.

With the doors of traditional culture shut in their faces, the wretched hordes could at least turn to sports. Catering to the carousing bachelor class in the big cities, sports of the late nineteenth century were barely a business. There were no stadiums or courts. Equipment and rules were improvised. Nobody dreamed of making a living or becoming famous. The distinction between competition and entertainment was blurry. At Tommy Norris's Livery Stable, a tavern in Lower Manhattan, a night's entertainment typically included a dog- or cockfight, rat-baiting, a bare-knuckle prizefight, a skirmish of billy goats, and a boxing match between two ladies wearing nothing but trunks.

Upstanding citizens were naturally offended by the "rowdyism, villainy, scoundrelism and boiled-down viciousness" of the fun and games. Soon, reformers tried to reclaim sports from the dissipations of the lower classes. In the era of the Muscular Christian, educators and clergy saw "physical culture" as an instrument of spiritual development. Others touted the lessons that sports taught in virile capitalism.

Whether promoting laissez-faire economics, religion, or massive corporate profits, once game-playing was seen as a means to another, higher, end and not an end in itself, it quickly lost much of its spontaneity. By the end of the twentieth century, intellectuals were according spectator sports a sort of high-church respectability. Boxing and baseball had acquired a certain snob appeal. To not treat athletes with religious reverence was to profane their sport. Meanwhile, the young men who shared Allen Iverson's or Latrell Sprewell's outlook on life were not sitting in the courtside seats with Spike and Woody. They likely could not even go to the game. Tickets had become too expensive. Held captive to marketing and advertising, to showmanship and spectacle, sports no longer belonged to the people. They belonged to the networks, to Nike and Reebok, to Budweiser and Gatorade. The devoted fan could still worship the gods of his idolatry. But they were now mediated gods whose marvels were experienced indirectly, through the prism of motives ulterior to the spirit of pure play.

WITH AN AUDIENCE of many millions spending billions of dollars a year, professional wrestling might not seem a pure and genuine expression of the romanticized "folk." Up until the early 1980s, though, dozens of small promotions throughout the United States, Canada, and Mexico operated in the spirit of tent revivals and traveling repertory companies. Promoters were more collaborators than competitors, generally respecting one another's territories. Sam Muchnick ran the biggest of these, the National Wrestling Alliance out of St. Louis. Verne Gagne worked a territory from Manitoba to Colorado. Don Owen had the Northwest. Stu Hart had the Canadian plains. Vince McMahon's dad had New York and Washington, as *his* father had before him. The Graham brothers had Florida. Cowboy Bob Kelly ran Alabama and Mississippi. And Dory Funk ruled Texas, except for Houston, which belonged to Paul Boesch, and Dallas, where Fritz Von Erich ruled the roost.

Although they have lost their kingdoms, many of these men are still around, showing up at reunions to reminisce about wrestling's golden age, which came to an end when Jess McMahon's punk grandson Vince Jr. and his whip-smart wife Linda came along and, one by one, put them all out of business. Hardly without guile themselves, the old-timers nevertheless wax nostalgic for the business's lost innocence, back when they still insisted—and people still believed—that wrestling, like

Santa Claus, was real. What they really miss, I think, is the opportunity to indulge their own rascality. Not quite crooks, they weren't ever going to be considered reputable businessmen, either. They didn't have to know anything about merchandizing or licensing. Terms like "synergy," "core competencies," and "revenue streams" never entered their vocabulary. They were just small-time cigar-chomping hustlers, trying to make a fast buck. But it was a playful con that harmed nobody.

Enter Vincent Kennedy McMahon, Jr. Born 1945. Parents divorced. Raised by mother in North Carolina trailer park. An abusive stepfather. Sexual weirdness (if not abuse) by mother. Didn't meet father until twelve years old. Dyslexic, a discipline problem; shipped off to Fishbourne Military School in Virginia. Married and expecting son Shane when graduating from East Carolina University. Sold Sweetheart paper cups before father let him promote wrestling in Bangor, Maine. He and wife Linda bought out father in 1982. Quickly set about invading other promoters' regional territories. Big on family values, despite story lines and infidelities. Considers himself "a giver." Considers wrestling the "highest form of entertainment." Says he hates liars and half-truths. Thinks communication should be visceral. Says: "A big kick in the nuts is always primo." Says: "I am of the people." Says: "My job is to entertain the masses at whatever level they want."

Though he would be the one to bust the trust, McMahon wasn't the first promoter to take wrestling national. After buying the low-powered UHF Atlanta television station WJRJ in 1971, Ted Turner needed to fill airtime with cheap programming, something professional wrestling had always provided. For the local stations, wrestling had always come virtually free of charge. After the DuMont network went off the air, promoters had been mailing off tapes of shows gratis as a way of advertising upcoming live shows. The only difference between the two hours of southern-style grappling that Turner aired every Saturday afternoon and what you saw on your local television station was that his "Superstation that serves the nation" broadcast via satellite to the whole country. Qualitatively, however, there was no difference. Soon, more networks came on the scene, but since most homes still were not wired for cable in the early 1980s, they were mainly interested in filling airtime at minimal expense. Any schlock would do, and the McMahons were only too happy to provide it, giving wrestling a foothold in the rapidly expanding cable market.

The three big wrestling booms have coincided with the advent of new communication technology: television itself in the late 1940s, cable and pay-per-view thirty years later, and the Internet in the mid-1990s. But 1984 was the pivotal year in wrestling's development from chump-change cultural oddity to national phenomenon. The year before, Vince McMahon had bought the company from his father. World *Wide* Wrestling Federation (as the company was then called) had not been part of the National Wrestling Alliance consortium, whose promoters met once a year to coordinate their efforts. Still, Vincent McMahon, Sr., respected its codes, unlike his son, who immediately began encroaching on other promoters' territories—for instance, stealing from Verne Gagne the services of a curiously charismatic wrestler named Terry "The Boulder" Bollea (Hulk Hogan) and from Don Owen another cleft-chinned balding blond named James Janos (Jesse Ventura).

Then Cyndi Lauper entered the picture. Meeting Captain Lou Albano on an airplane, the pop singer asked the old wrestling manager with safety pins piercing his cheek to play her father in one of MTV's first, and most successful, music videos, "Girls Just Wanna Have Fun." MTV's *Brawl to Settle It All*—a wrestling/variety show revolving around Lauper and Albano in a camped-up father-daughter feud—created an unexpected media frisson. Wrestling now had the hipster's seal of approval. And soon, with *20/20*'s John Stossel getting slapped upside the head for calling the business fake and comedian Richard Belzer passing out under Hogan's sleeper hold, it was getting something even more valuable: heat.

Unlike Turner and other media executives who were merely using wrestling out of convenience as a stepping-stone to bigger and better broadcasting ambitions (CNN was built on the backs of wrestlers), McMahon was wholly committed to the business, the only one whose fortunes rose and . . . well, kept rising on America's seemingly insatiable appetite for belligerence and buffoonery.

DESPITE—or maybe because of—the half-assed quality of the productions, the independent companies still attracted intensely loyal fans, diehards who rejected the bigger national promotions on staunch principle. "Like a lot of wrestling fans, I consider myself a free spirit, and I don't want to be told how to live my life," David O'Gorman said during a show at a community rec center in Staten Island. A short, chunky man with arrestingly pale blue eyes, O'Gorman made a point of only wearing black T-shirts and black sweatpants to wrestling events in case the show was broadcast on a cable-access channel. Black clothes, he believed, made him look thinner. Stepping outside to have a cigarette, we talked about his luxurious mullet haircut, which he never stopped combing, about the Son of Sam, who was once a neighbor in Yonkers, and about the evils of the federal government. An avowed libertarian, O'Gorman believed that WWE typified the perniciousness of the establishment and therefore would only pay to see independent promotions.

"That's just a general philosophy," he explained. "I don't want to be told what to wear, what to buy, what to eat, what to watch, or who to admire. I don't care if it's the mass media, religion, or government—everything is a controlling technique. It's to keep the masses sedate."

O'Gorman had advanced views on many subjects, and when he and I and his teenage son, Nicholas, drove out to a show in Mineola, Long Island, a few weeks later, I kept losing his train of thought. Aliens had contributed to his spiritual growth, making him more alert to fraud and manipulation, he told me. "First there was the Roswell landing in 1947," he said. "And the next year, Harry Truman was elected president—you know what I'm saying?"

"But wait," I said. "Truman became president when Roosevelt died—in 1945, I think."

"Exactly. And then the CIA was created in 1948."

" . . . ?"

"And when Marilyn Monroe died, they sent a copy of her autopsy to the head of the Air Force in charge of UFO investigations. See what I'm saying?"

I said, "Was Marilyn Monroe a . . . ?"

"An alien? No. But somebody wanted to shut her up."

There was a point to this, I believe, and it related to wrestling. Unlike some things in the modern world, O'Gorman was telling me, clandestine forces had not imposed professional wrestling on the people.

At the same time, though, wrestling's phenomenal popularity was cause for worry. Specifically, O'Gorman feared that
this wonderful thing he and Nicholas had helped create might
become too classy and commercial—and leave them behind.
Again and again, fans used the word "pure" to describe indie
companies like ECW. They didn't mean that the matches
weren't scripted or the victories predetermined, or even that

the ratio of meaningless blather to meaningful wrestling wasn't high. They meant, simply, that the banalizing effects of the profit motive had not entirely polluted their experience. Few would have put it in just those terms. They wouldn't have said they were protesting a culture of manufactured desires and manipulated emotions. They had none of the arrogant self-consciousness of college-educated erstwhile slackers exorcising their oedipal conflicts against the makers of sneakers and specialty coffee. They weren't artists, activists, anarchists, environmentalists, feminists, lefties, poets, pranksters, punks, provocateurs, or rabble-rousers. They were innocents, simply looking to be entertained. Sitting at home listening to reverential sports announcers eliciting empty platitudes from prima donna athletes no longer did it for them. They wanted a total theatrical experience of the kind that the French actor, playwright, and certified madman Antonin Artaud conceived in the 1920s—a theater that eliminated the distance between audience and performer and evoked the forbidden pleasures of ancient tribal festivals. Not that they were quoting Artaud's theories on the theater of cruelty and the destruction of bourgeois art. But Artaud and Heyman were birds of a feather. It was a rare ECW fight, for example, that didn't spill out of the ring, over the metal barricades, and into the crowd. At a show in Florida, hundreds of fans piled into the eighteen-by-eighteen-foot ring before it collapsed. In a match with Mick Foley (Mankind), Terry Funk asked a fan to lend him his metal folding chair; by the time Foley and Funk had escaped to the locker room, more than four hundred chairs had been thrown in the ring.

"A WWE show is more like going to a movie," Urial Yakobov explained on one of his bus trips. "They're putting on a show *for* you, which is different than if you are part of the show. Fans chanting 'Show Your Tits!' or 'She's a Crack Whore!' and stuff like that—that's what you can do at an indie show. And I love it. There is nothing like it, especially when I feel like I'm one of the leaders. Most things, you just sit there. You watch it on TV. The only thing you can do is change the channel. But here you're acting along with the wrestlers. You're providing entertainment to everybody, to the person sitting next to you, to the person across the arena. To tell you the truth, we're providing as much entertainment as the wrestlers in the ring."

But maintaining that Rabelaisian atmosphere was not easy under the onslaught of consumerism. By the time I started going to ECW shows, most of the company's biggest stars (such as Mankind, Steve Austin, Taz, and The Dudley Boyz) had gone on to much bigger fame at WWE and WCW, taking the ECW attitude with them.

It was the old story of mass culture appropriating the fresh ideas of a subculture. Facing serious competition from Turner's WCW after a long and costly investigation for assorted crimes and misdemeanors,[*] McMahon took the rebellious, antiestablishment, in-your-face swagger that Gordon, Heyman & Associates had created in partnership with fans like Urial

---

[*] An ex-wrestler was accused of coercing ring boys into sex. McMahon himself was accused of raping a secretary. Those allegations went no further than the court of public disgrace, as adjudicated by the honorable Geraldo Rivera. And despite the testimony of dozens of wrestlers that McMahon pressured them to "go on the gas," a federal jury found him not guilty of conspiring to distribute steroids. Still, the expense of mounting a legal defense had taken its toll on the company.

Yakobov in the dank and fetid atmosphere of small-time wrestling venues and then repackaged it for sale to the entire country in a brand he called "WWE Attitude." Instead of experiencing an attitude, that is, fans were now able to buy it, in the form of bobblehead dolls.

Not that anyone was complaining. World Wrestling Entertainment had created a semireligious fervor revolving around an iconography of gaudy grandeur. To attend a live show, particularly the monthly pay-per-view events or its annual WrestleMania extravaganza, was to have an almost transcendental experience in consumer capitalism. "This is bigger than life, and my own life is, well, smaller than life," is how Brandy Hall, a grocery-store cashier, summed up her WrestleMania experience in Houston. Two days before the following year's extravaganza in Toronto's SkyDome, Jason Snider listed the pilgrimage as one of his top three life goals. "The other two are still blank," he said.

It is tempting to say that the ploy involved underhanded manipulation. As personified by Vince McMahon, however, WWE made no pretense to being anything other than what it so obviously was—manipulative, opportunistic, and deceptive, the model postindustrial company in an economy no longer based on the making of things but merely the marketing of them. When I visited WWE's headquarters in Stamford, Connecticut, the subject of wrestling never once came up. It was simply called "the product" or "the content." "We are about branding—that's what we do," Linda McMahon told me, the implication being that wrestling hardly mattered in the scheme of their larger ambitions. Like P. T. Barnum, her husband understood that, rather than resent the con, the public felt flattered by the lengths to which anyone would go to sucker them.

At any rate, that was the conclusion Dave Larson and his eighteen-year-old daughter Karen came to at Toronto's WrestleMania. They had traveled eight hours by bus from Timmons, Ontario, an expense of $125 apiece. Larson, a miner, had also paid $280 for floor seating. "We saved up—this was our Christmas present," he told me. "It was more than we could afford but we decided to splurge. I'd have paid anything for these tickets." He had to admit, though, that the show was a disappointment. Proximity to the ring somehow didn't translate into the immediacy they had hoped for. "When you can't see the Jumbotron," he said, "it's not right in your face like they said it would be."

Even so, just knowing that his wife was recording the pay-per-view, and that he and Karen had been part of it—and would be able to watch it later on TV—seemed to make it all worthwhile. "It's still the WWE," he said, "and we love the WWE."

So did millions of others. WWE's ratings had doubled less than a year after copping ECW's attitude. Profits went from minus $6.5 million in 1997 to $56 million in 1999. Nineteen ninety-seven saw only twenty-five newspaper and magazine articles mentioning professional wrestling; by 1999, the interest had increased tenfold. And so had the McMahon family's fortunes. By 2001, the McMahons were billionaires, and ECW was struggling for survival.

# CHAPTER FOUR

WHO KNOWS IN THIS LIFE OF OURS WHAT IS REALLY TRUE AND WHAT IS ENCHANTING MAKE-BELIEVE?    —ZSA ZSA GABOR

AN YOU IMAGINE the level of a mind that watches wrestling?" a crabby elitist played by Max von Sydow asks in Woody Allen's *Hannah and Her Sisters*. The cover stories and think pieces that pro wrestling received at its peak of popularity weren't quite that dismissive. With the ascendance of Vince McMahon and WWE, superiority now took the form of condescending fascination. Confessing a fondness for professional wrestling was a sign of one's advanced camp sensibility. Except to demonstrate how perfectly droll they could be, however, the mainstream commentators had no more interest than Woody Allen did in understanding why pro wrestling meant so much to so many people. Wrestlers were happy fools—they couldn't possibly have anything interesting to say, not like poets or performance artists, right?

Well, not so fast. Cultural theorists are forever going on about sites of gender struggles. By "sites" they usually mean some broad category, like fashion or advertising, not an actual location. And by "struggles" they're generally referring to subtle "modes of resistance" and not a literal, physical fight. We have become consumers of illusions, they say; modern life has become an endless circuit of simulacra; at a certain level nothing is certain; truth is always subjective; etc.

The ideas seem abstruse and highfalutin. But it is just this sort of thing that preoccupies wrestlers and their fans. For them, the squared circle of the wrestling ring really is a site of their struggles with the difficulties of living in complex and confusing times. At a glance, the fantasies of professional wrestling seem to simplify the complexity by reducing everything to neat oppositions. But ultimately it only raises new and even more confounding questions. Where does fantasy end and reality begin? Where does the performance stop and life take over? And is there a point where it no longer matters? If you are bleeding, who cares whether you are operating in the realm of fantasy or reality? You are still bleeding.

Wrestling is a form of what has been called "deep play"— an activity that defies common sense, bringing more pain to its participants than pleasure. To see young men with dollar bills staple-gunned to their faces, with shards of glass embedded in their scalps, with flesh torn in a hundred places from barbed wire, most people would naturally conclude there was some

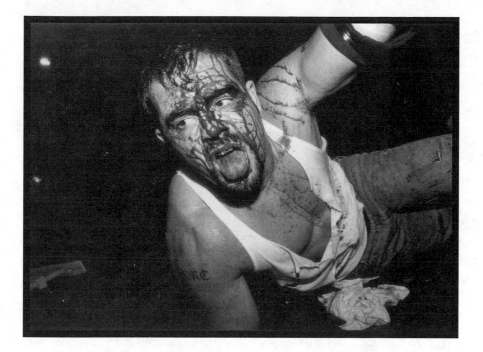

MATT PRINCE, AKA WIFEBEATER

sort of sickness at work here. And, in fact, many wrestlers are suffering in one way or another, but the mayhem they subject themselves to in the ring is seldom the cause or the most worrisome effect of their troubles. Even the healthiest and happiest of hardcore professional wrestlers subject themselves to suffering that cannot be justified by a cost-benefit analysis.

Why? In a well-known essay on the "deep play" of the Balinese cockfight, the cultural anthropologist Clifford Geertz suggests an answer:

> What it does is what, for other peoples with other temperaments and other conventions, *King Lear* and *Crime and Punishment* do; it catches up

themes . . . and, ordering them into an encompass-
ing structure, presents them in such a way as to
throw into relief a particular view of their essential
nature. It puts a construction on them, makes
them, to those historically positioned to appreciate
the construction, meaningful—visible, tangible,
graspable—"real," in an ideational sense.

For some reason, though, we're a lot quicker to see meaning and importance in the popular rites of people from distant
times and places than we are in the stuff of our own culture.

MERICA, perhaps more than any other country, has
been vexed by popular culture, in part because we have
so much of it, but also because it often tests our democratic ideals. A century after Walt Whitman hailed a
culture of "the average, the bodily, the concrete, the
democratic, the popular," even commentators with Commu-
nist political sympathies were feeling exasperated by the tastes
of the lumpen-proletariat. Folk art was one thing, the thinking went: it was innocent, untainted by commercialism, the
product of ancient traditions, the work of honest artisans. . . .
Popular culture was something else altogether: vulgar, manipulative, depersonalized, appealing to the lowest common de-
nominator. To the "ignoramuses"—as Dwight Macdonald
referred to the fans of popular entertainment—the culture
must bow. The average man "plays the same role the child
plays in the American home," Macdonald quotes fellow au-

thor Mary McCarthy as saying. "He is an inferior being who must nevertheless be propitiated."

The fretting of mid-century intellectuals wasn't categorical. T. S. Eliot had a taste for music-hall comedians. Irving Howe admired the "folk spontaneity" of baseball. Robert Warshow admitted that *Mad* magazine was not necessarily the ruin of young minds. And, of course, a number of writers have been eager to show they're no girlie-men by waxing macho about boxing. Even so, there was little serious consideration that the cultural concerns of millions of ordinary Americans were worth bothering to comprehend. As the critic Leslie Fiedler observed: "The notion that there is more than one language of art, or rather, that there is something not quite art, which performs art's function for most men in our society, is disquieting enough for anyone, and completely unacceptable to the sentimental egalitarian."*

The prospect of a wrestling promotion receiving the sort of arts funding that sustains even the most half-assed dance or

---

*A 1990 exhibit mounted at the Museum of Modern Art supposedly signaled a new receptiveness to mass tastes. Titled *High and Low: Modern Art and Popular Culture*, the show juxtaposed advertisements and comic strips next to the standard examples of "high" art. You'll hear critics refer to some cultural discussion as "post–*High and Low*," as if the exhibit heralded an opened-arm acceptance of pop culture. In fact, its curators were only interested in reaffirming the same old hierarchy. Others, however, had begun paying attention to popular culture, from pornography to romance novels. All too often, though, the critical acrobatics were in the service of an exalted ideology. All the while, the usual arty malarkey continued to enjoy intellectual and cultural sanction. "Art is what you can get away with," said Andy Warhol, and it turned out you could get away with pretty much anything, so long as you called it art.

theatrical companies is, I suppose, ludicrous. (Wrestling, to its credit, is impervious to elitist humbug.) Yet I was beginning to see that there was a kind of witless genius to professional wrestling, so perfectly did it dramatize the preoccupations and pathologies of society. Through speech, song, and dance, pro wrestling spoke to matters of broad and compelling interest. It performed art's function: it said the right things at the right time in the right way to the right people.

To fully appreciate this, you had to look beyond the antics in the ring. The gymnastics were, as the great dance critic Edwin Denby said of ballet, "absurd by nature," of interest not for any great intellectual substance but simply for the pleasure of watching bodies in motion. But that was just one small aspect of the spectacle. The drama also spilled over into the lives of the wrestlers. Both onstage and off, both in and out of costume, wrestlers delivered their lines and performed their parts in what often turned out to be a sad travesty of personal ambition. Their preposterous arrogance was meant to point up the absurd self-importance of other types of celebrities. Likewise, their campy machismo was meant to be a grotesque of male vanity. And everyone, fans and performers alike, was supposed to be collaborating in the farce. Amazingly, though, it was the rare wrestler who saw his performance as a send-up of manliness, celebrity, or anything else. Somewhere along the line, the ridiculousness became ridiculously real. Wrestlers forgot that they were play-acting and began taking their roles seriously. They not only took themselves seriously as acrobatic comic performers, they also regarded the matches as testaments to their own magnificence. Cast in the role of swaggering he-men, they'd strut around insisting that friends call them Macho Man, or whatever. If they beat up men in the ring, they beat up strangers in bars—or, just as often, went too far and took a beating themselves. They'd assault police officers. They'd slap their wives around. They'd brag about winning some intercontinental world television junior light heavyweight belt for a promotion nobody had ever heard of, as if it meant anything. Eventually, as their alter egos took over, they'd lose contact with any kind of authentic identity. After years of bodybuilding and steroid abuse, they'd have metamorphosed into something strange and new.

"It's incredible to watch," Joanie Laurer told me soon after she quit her job in the WWE as Chyna, the biggest female star in wrestling history. "The wrestlers want the fantasy to be real. They get lost in it. They believe their own shit and get consumed with wanting to be the most magnificent person on the planet—not realizing their fame was given to them by Vince McMahon. Then they fall and don't know who they are anymore. It's a real slap in the face."

For the fans, however, the spectacle of men caught between fantasy and reality made for a theater even more riveting than the agonies and ecstasies that wrestlers pretended to in the ring. Soon promoters took the hint. Rejecting "the same old simplistic theory of good guys against bad guys," as McMahon put it, the business began to embrace a crude psychological realism in the 1990s. To really get over with fans, wrestlers now had to tap into their inner demons and become one with their characters, like method actors. They did not just play sociopaths, they became them. The wrestling in the ring was still as fake as ever, but the psychodramas that it alluded to often were not. When McMahon interviewed a deranged Brian Pillman at his home in Kentucky, for example, fans knew that Flyin' Brian's psychotic routine was only partly an act. His aiming a 9mm Glock pistol at Stone Cold Steve Austin while shouting (between commercials for children's toys), "Get the hell out of the fucking way"—yes, that was more or less scripted. The part about being injured and hopped up on drugs after having crashed his Humvee, how-ever—that was real. That was Brian being Brian, a half-cocked scrapper who had survived thirty-one operations for throat cancer to walk his way on to the Cincinnati Bengals before turning to wrestling. Once, while working for ECW, Pillman had to be stopped from pissing in the ring. He was sometimes so medicated on Vicodin and Percocets that, when he ate, he couldn't find his mouth. But so long as the arrests, the re-straining orders, and the failed drug tests kept people talking about him, Pillman didn't mind everyone thinking he was los-ing it. That was the con, and Pillman more than anyone was taken in by it. He'd become a mark for himself, as fans say—until, in the ultimate perfection of his suicidal iconography, he was found dead in a Budget-tel motel, from an apparent drug overdose, at the age of thirty-five.

A T LEAST he would have a lot of company. In a five-year period, some sixty wrestlers died under the age of forty-five. Nevertheless, despite the risks to body and soul, young men all over the country felt it was their duty as Americans to pursue this dream of per-sonal glory.

Wrestlers hail from all parts of the globe. In Japan and Mexico and India, the wrestlers Rikidozan, Mil Mascaras, and Dara Singh are probably as emblematic of their countries' cultural values as Hulk Hogan has been to ours. The English town of Wigan, between Liverpool and Manchester, is famous for its tradition of straight-up submission wrestling. For a time in the 1980s, the Dallas-based World Class Championship Wrestling produced the most popular television show in Israel, despite the promoter's born-again Christian pieties. More recently, native Aymara and Quechua women, wearing traditional bowler hats and ample skirts, have taken to the ring in Bolivia—the "fighting Cholitas," they're called. And with the advent of the Internet, fans from Hunan to Tehran have been able to keep up with the careers of even obscure jobbers in the dinkiest independent promotion.

Still, professional wrestling is especially appealing to a country with a deep faith in self-invention, in new beginnings—a faith conveyed through the myths of popular culture. I'm talking about the myth of the pioneer, the frontiersman, the cowboy, the lone ranger, the avenging comic-book superhero, able to change form in an instant, the myth of the self-made man, the man-on-the-make, the gambler, the gangster, and the gunslinger. What all of these mythopoeic figures of pop culture have in common is a deeply held American belief in rebirth, no matter how dangerous. The myth of regeneration through violence, historian Richard Slotkin contends, has been "the structuring metaphor of the American experience"—even today, when most men work cooperatively with others and experience adventure not of necessity but as an expensive sport. It is no coincidence, for example, that around the time many nineteenth-century social commentators were remarking on the feminization of America, the brutal sport of boxing captured the public's imagination, beginning an era that has been fairly obsessed with athletics. The bouts weren't rehearsed or predetermined (bare-knuckle fights often went more than a hundred rounds, sometimes ending in death). But the spectacle of confining two men who had no personal grudge to a small ring and having them beat each other senseless was nevertheless a staged affair—a ritual performance, articulating collective ideals of male will. Neither honor nor property nor political power was at stake. Something else was, though—manliness.

Taking a Freudian approach, one might say that the two-fisted he-stuff of blood sports was a "reaction-formation" to castration anxieties. That's the interpretation anthropologists have often applied to the brutal rites of so-called primitive people. Certainly pro wrestling, with its constant attention to phallic power interrupted by commercials for erectile-dysfunction drugs, seems designed to assuage such fears. But you don't have to go there (and, really, who wants to?) to see sports' emphasis on the human body as an antidote to the massive technological, economic, and demographic changes that have fundamentally unmanned men in the last 150 years. Elaborately conceived, often tedious, and ultimately inconsequential, sports nevertheless salvaged a disgraced manhood. Throwing down a slam dunk or exulting in the end zone gave men an opportunity to feel once again triumphant.

The reality remained, though, that very few men had the opportunity, let alone the ability, to rip a fastball out of the park. As Frederick Exley writes in *A Fan's Notes*, it is the sorry fate of most men to "sit in the stands . . . and acclaim others." When most young men come to this crushing realization, they don't try to compensate by lacerating their flesh with a gasoline-powered weed whacker. They take up golf or tennis and wage their status struggles in other socially accepted ways. But what was true in 1960, when the social critic Paul Goodman observed that despite its abundant wealth the United States was still "lacking in enough man's work," is even truer today. Young American men, Goodman concluded, find themselves at a difficult juncture of psychological development: they're too old to simply play. But there is nothing else to which they can give themselves with such "fierce intensity." So they continue to play, absurdly.

In the past, boys looked to their fathers to guide them toward a sense of purpose. In the 1990s, however, as the traditional roles they'd once performed were taken away from them, a lot of older men seemed to have lost the manhood script. Desperate to find a new one, they marched by the millions in empowerment rallies. They flocked to woodsy retreats to sing, dance, and weep. They gathered in "anger-management" groups, where they learned to love themselves. They packed football stadiums at sixty dollars a pop, chanting, "Power, power, we got the power!" as football-coaches-turned-evangelists exhorted them to reclaim their manhood. They read periodicals like *New Man*, which told them there was "more to being a man than being a breadwinner," and books such as Gordon Dalbey's *Fight Like a Man*, which explained how to become "kingdom warriors."

It was Bill Moyers' PBS special *A Gathering of Men* that got the men's movement going, making a minor celebrity of Robert Bly, a white-haired poet and workshop guru who wasn't embarrassed to be seen wearing needlepoint vests. Abandoned by abusive and ineffectual fathers, captive to smothering mothers and demeaned by empowered women, the adult American male feels diminished and impotent, Bly reported in his bestselling *Iron John*. His solution: Go with the Wild Man! He will teach you not only to "write poetry and go out and sit by the ocean," but also that you don't "have to be on top all the time in sex anymore."

Poetry, the seashore, nontraditional sex . . . Rereading these passages, I couldn't wait to get back to the chair-throwing in Viking Hall. If nothing else, the mook culture of hardcore wrestling, Howard Stern, and Johnny Knoxville had a sense of humor. And its apostles certainly didn't need to go searching for that "wet and muddy portion" of themselves, as Bly advised. They had never lost it.

Bly reported that it was "clear to men that the images of adult manhood given by the popular culture are worn out." Turns out, he would wear out his welcome quicker than the "defective" macho mythologies he disparaged. He and his disciples might not have known what to make of Sylvester Stallone, say, but millions of young men, identifying with Rocky's or Rambo's obvious insecurities, had known exactly how to read him. And regardless of whether they or he could put it in words, another generation of young men understood what The Rock was telling them, too. Rambo and Rocky said you had to fight through your insecurities for your manhood. The Rock said that, too. But he also said something else—that in the end, manhood was a performance, a put-on.

Before I spoke to The Rock about this, I would talk to hundreds of other wrestlers, most of whom weren't and never would be famous. They were "professional" in name only, making almost no money for their efforts. Like the lost souls that turn up in Luigi Pirandello's great play *Six Characters in*

*Search of an Author*, they carried an important drama within them, and they desperately wanted to bring that drama to life. Whether they should turn out to be a hero to anyone's life but their own, or whether that station would be held by someone else, hardly mattered in my opinion.

# CHAPTER FIVE

> TO GIVE TO MEN THAT PORTION OF HOPE AND ILLUSION WITHOUT WHICH THEY CANNOT LIVE, SUCH IS THE REASON FOR THE EXISTENCE OF GODS, HEROES, AND POETS.
>
> —DANIEL LESUEUR

O NE DAY," The Rock would tell himself, bucking up his resolve in a moment of disappointment and defeat, "I'm going to make my mark in this world."

In a more heroic age, The Rock might have tried to vindicate himself in combat or, if there were no wars to be fought, in a duel or in the prizefighting ring. Boxing conveyed the nobility of single combat, the practice from the pre-Christian era of pitting two men, instead of whole armies, against each other. After the ritualistic weigh-in and prefight stare-down, the boxers were stripped of all vanity and, in the best of fights, of all but the last vestiges of ego. They were just two bodies in extremis fighting for survival. It was real, unscripted, unrehearsed, unambiguous. Either you won or you lost. There was no escaping the confines of the ring. There were no last-second "run-ins" from well-connected associates. Knowing how to win friends and influence people was of no consequence. Irony and wit got you nowhere. For writers and filmmakers, the ordeals of boxing provided a useful sieve for distilling mythic lessons in manliness and valor.

The inanities of professional wrestling would seem to offer instruction of another order. Not the noble savages fighting for their living in the "old, primitive, royal, animal way," as Jack London puts it in his classic story "A Piece of Steak," pro wrestlers were conspicuously ignoble savages, hustling themselves in distinctly modern ways.

To thousands of young men, that hustle was anything but humiliating. It was ennobling. Never mind that professional wrestlers played pretend for a living, or that most Americans would rather take a chair shot than watch one. The seven million households that did regularly watch the Monday-night wrestling broadcasts somehow legitimated the prestige of the professional wrestler for the rest of us. He was supposed to be a mock star, a parody of celebrity narcissism. Yet he was taken for the real thing—an important person. So long as these men were known to somebody, they seemed justified in their splendor. Suddenly, they were on the covers of serious news magazines. Their memoirs were bestsellers. They spoke at political conventions. Jesse Ventura (a man who, as governor of Minnesota, liked to get "camouflaged up, lock and load," and go on "sneaky-crawl, [Navy] SEAL-style" pretend special-op patrols) was mentioned as a possible presidential candidate. It wasn't that anyone really took wrestling seriously. It was that nobody took much of anything seriously and were therefore happy to embrace "excrement as worthy of their attention, and direct the enthusiasm of their fellows to excrement," as George W. S. Trow writes in *Within the Context of No Context*.

Understanding the penchant for manifest crap was no simple matter. In 2005, a Princeton philosophy professor's painstaking exegesis of the matter, *On Bullshit*, rose to the very top of the *New York Times* bestseller list, in part because, even though its author resists the temptation, a reader can't help but find some obvious examples in American society, in politics in particular. Bullshit, as Professor Harry Frankfurt defines it, isn't so much a lie or a deception as it is a total disregard for truth and fact, for "how things really are." For bullshit to fly, it needs not just the active agency of the bullshitter but, more importantly, a receptive audience equally uninterested in truth.

Understandably, the ubiquitous humbug confused an awful lot of young people anxiously searching for their own significance. If the country's major investment banks couldn't be bothered to question the sham profits of Enron, for example, why should teenage boys second-guess the fabricated prestige of professional wrestlers? If *Newsweek* magazine couldn't tell the difference, how were they to be expected to distinguish between what got hyped and what was truly praiseworthy? "Doing all kinds of crazy stuff—you feel like a celebrity, you get noticed at the mall," Josh Piscura, a star of the backyard wrestling scene, told me. "It's pretty cool to be famous," said Liz Miklosi, a cheerful nineteen-year-old from Queens, New York, explaining why she hoped a boob job would get her on TV as a valet in WWE. "I mean, everybody likes famous people. Everybody looks up to them and stuff."

Liz was right. All celebrities were created more or less equal. "Of all Americans," says Trow, "only they are complete."

The reality was, though, that aspiring wrestlers seldom made any money to speak of. Very often they had to sell so many tickets just to get on the card. Yet that inconvenient fact, like the fact that a lot of them were just fat blobs barely able to climb into the ring, didn't keep them from feeling like stars.

"And if you're a star," promoters like Rob Zicari were telling them, "you're somebody. If you're not, if you're just another one of the two hundred and eighty-fucking million people in this country—you're nobody. It's that simple."

YOU DIDN'T have to tell that to Oren Hawxhurst, who wrestled for Zicari's Los Angeles–based promotion Xtreme Professional Wrestling. As a little boy growing up in the mixed-race trailer-park ghettos of New Orleans, Hawxhurst had made up his mind that wrestling would be his ticket out of a crap childhood. At twenty, he still was not much more than a boy, yet he had been living on his own, on the streets or with friends or in juvenile correctional centers, since he was eleven. He had a father who beat him and wanted nothing to do with him. He had a mother who went out every night, partying and fighting and bringing home men even worse than his dad. Then, at sixteen, Hawxhurst became a father himself, and soon after got married. Wanting to be a wrestler had kept him not quite on the straight and narrow, he figured, but it at least kept him from dying of a heroin overdose, as ten people he knew in high school had. Yet whenever he mentioned the ambition, his dad would only tell him that he would wind up a loser just like his mom. He listened to that for years, until the question finally occurred to him: What did his dad know about ambition? The guy hadn't ever done anything, except put him down. "Would it bug me if I ended up like him? Fuck, yeah," Hawxhurst told me after his first appearance in Viking Hall. "I'm not saying everybody has to be on TV and shit, but . . ."

But if he, personally, was looking to get over in this life, it was not as if Hawxhurst had a lot of options. He wasn't going to become a professor or a financier or a self-important journalist pontificating on TV. Experience told him that he didn't, and never would, belong to that kind of elite. Except for wrestling, he entertained no other possibilities for having a life he could be proud of. School was not his thing. Neither was sitting behind a desk. And he didn't see the point of getting his ass shot off in the military. He did have a way with the ladies, so maybe he could make a living as a porn star, he joked. For the time being, he took construction jobs that mostly involved crawling underneath houses in the sweltering Louisiana heat, but knowing that his father also worked in construction, as an electrician, pretty well killed any satisfaction he might have taken from that. And, anyway, it wasn't as if the jobs he could get held out any realistic promise of upward mobility; they didn't even offer health insurance. Even during the prosperous 1990s, with near full employment, the working poor had just gotten poorer and class lines had further solidified. For Hawxhurst, it seemed that only fame could catapult him out of a life of quiet desperation.

Tall and lithe, with pale white skin, piercing blue eyes, several menacing tattoos, and (for the moment) a shaved head, Hawxhurst was an arresting figure. He looked like a skinhead,

but a skinhead with intense feelings of civic pride. The "NOLA" tattooed across his abdomen? An acronym for his hometown, New Orleans, LA. The Croix de Fleury tattooed on the underside of his left arm? A tribute to the Saints, his favorite football team. And the number 5 0 4 above it? His area code.

As a kid, Hawxhurst went to every show that came anywhere near New Orleans, always hanging around the arena afterwards, hoping to get his picture taken with a wrestler. After an ECW show, he got up the courage to initiate a conversation with the wrestler Vic Grimes, who played a menacing badass in the tag team known as the Baldies. "I was scared to talk to him," Hawxhurst told me. "He looked like a real bad dude. A lot of wrestlers are assholes. But he ended up being very, very cool. I told him I wanted to be a professional wrestler. He said keep in touch. So I did. I sent him a video, and he called from Los Angeles and said, 'Damn, dude! You got a hell of a lot of potential. I can teach you a lot!' I was so jacked! The wrestling around New Orleans ain't shit. I was working for a lot of independent companies I didn't even know the names of, driving ten hours to shows in Texas or Florida or wherever just to work for free, to get ring experience. But I wasn't learning nothing. So when Vic said, 'Bring your stuff to L.A., bring your wife, bring your son, and I'll train you,' I said, 'Screw this, if I don't move, I ain't ever going to make it.' I had about two thousand dollars saved up.

"My wife—her name is Karen—she was very supportive. She stands by her man. She's a senior in college now. Next year she's going to medical school. She's always gotten straight A's her whole life. She said, 'Baby, I know this is what you've always wanted to do. Why don't I just drop out of school for a year and get a job.' I said, 'Baby, there's no way I'm going to let you drop out of school.' So I moved out on my own for a while, and she came in the summer, and then we moved back.

"I always had three goals in life. I wanted to get married and have a kid. I wanted to get my high school diploma. And I wanted to be a professional wrestler. There was nothing else I really wanted to be in life. People were always, like, 'You need a backup plan.' And I'm always, 'No, I don't—I'm going to be a wrestler.' "

But despite his abundant enthusiasm and the encouragement he was getting from more experienced wrestlers, Hawxhurst was finding that the doors to his dreams, while not exactly closed, did not lead anywhere. He had a gimmick— appearing in a white satin clerical smock, he was known as Altar Boy Luke—and if he was willing to bloody himself in a so-called death match, he sometimes even got paid, enough anyway that he felt he could legitimately call himself a "professional" wrestler. Still, it was depressing to admit that he still had not gotten over with anyone but his grandmother.

W HEN I BEGAN going to wrestling shows, I thought I would meet a lot of young men without fathers, looking for lessons on how to be a man. And I did. Most of the boys on Urial Yakobov's bus trips said they had no relationship with their fathers. "Don't have one, don't want one" was the general attitude. It was a different story with their mothers. "I'm a mama's boy," one fan wrote on a questionnaire. "She's my pal," said another.

"She's very special to me, I tell her everything." Another said: "My mom cares about me a lot; our relationship is definitely the best it could be. We take care of each other and get along amazingly." And although an ECW show, with its references to sluts and whores, was not the sort of place you'd want to bring your mom, a lot of mothers did come to Viking Hall. They weren't fans. They came because their sons didn't have fathers to take them. "I play mother and dad both," said Terri Barnett, who had flown up one weekend from Beaumont, Texas, with her fourteen-year-old son Bucky. A psychiatric nurse, she had been going to hardcore shows ever since her husband had walked out three years earlier. "I do the things that I think a dad should do, to the best of my ability, so he doesn't turn out to be a mama's boy."

But I had to be careful about making sweeping generalizations about absent fathers, because I had also met men like Joe Joe Russello and David O'Gorman, who were deeply involved in their sons' lives. It turned out, too, that many of my conversations with wrestlers touched on fathering, specifically on their wanting to correct the neglect, in some cases the abuse, that they had known as boys.

Getting together with the wrestler James Fullington the morning after one of his epic drinking binges that ended with him dropping his pants in the ring, pouring beer down the blouse of a fifteen-year-old girl, and getting officially banned from wrestling in the state of Pennsylvania, I had hoped to talk about the dissolute direction he and so many wrestlers had taken in their lives. Fullington was not the type of guy to admit to being ashamed, but I got the feeling he was, especially since his three children had been on hand for the debauched performance. At age thirty-nine, he had recently separated from his

TERRI AND BUCKY BARNETT

wife. He mentioned seeing a psychiatrist, hoping she could help him understand why he drank so much (weekends that he wrestled, he'd start drinking Friday morning and wouldn't stop, not even to sleep, until he got home Sunday night); and he spoke of wanting to finally get his act together, not so much for his sake but his kids'. "We get lost in la-la land," he said as his three-year-old son Oliver lolled about the kitchen floor, keeping us company. "We act like we're these fucking superheroes, just because we're on fucking TV. It's such a crock of shit. It's not even a fucking job. The guy who lives in the fucking projects and has to go out to a job that he fucking hates because he's got kids that he's gotta feed—that's a fucking hero."

"Dad?" Oliver interrupted. "Dad, when I get bigger, can I say bad words?"

"What's that? Yeah, when you get bigger. Oliver, who's my best friend?"

"I am!" Oliver said, sidling up to this dad.

"What concerns me right now," Fullington went on, "is me and this kid being best friends. That's it. My parents never came to my ball games. I was a latchkey kid. We never went on vacation. It's not like I was abused or anything; it just wasn't the greatest childhood. They just weren't around. And that's not the way it's going to be with this kid. I'll do anything for him."

OREN HAWXHURST also spoke of wanting to be the sort of father to his son Perry that his own dad hadn't ever been to him. As a professional wrestler, he believed, he could be that man. At the same time it seemed that he, like a lot of young wrestlers I met, was still looking to find a father figure for himself, someone strong yet warm,

93

92

manly yet nurturing, who could show him what it meant to be a man in a world of image and artifice.

"It's tough, it's macho," he once said of wrestling's appeal. "It gives you the feeling of being masculine."

Professionally, Hawxhurst's prospects were depressing but not altogether hopeless. Most of the rough-and-tumble old-timers of wrestling's golden age had come from next to nothing, fleeing wasted dustbowl farms and the menial labor of the Depression. They were orphans and runaways and street hustlers who lived by their wits and made the most of an opportunity while it lasted. Roddy Piper had been living on the streets, getting by on panhandling and petty thievery. And now look at him: he wasn't winning Oscars, but with an eighth-grade education he'd done better than he could playing bagpipes—another trick he somehow learned as a boy.

Hawxhurst was proud of having read only two books in his entire life, both of them wrestling biographies. He was not alone. A couple of these books topped off the *New York Times* bestseller list. Wrestling fans swore by them, having discovered archetypal narratives that resonated with their own longings. Though chock-full of self-promoting pap, they are fundamentally stories of self-discovery and self-achievement. During a period of personal crisis ("I was down but not out"), the hero suddenly decides to become a professional wrestler ("I knew in my heart that I had found my calling"). Upon reflection, he realizes this has always been his destiny ("there was a force guiding my life that was bigger than coincidence"), only self-doubt has kept him from pursing it ("I was getting so used to people calling me stupid that I was starting to believe it"). Now that he has answered the call, nothing can deter him ("Whatever it took, I was going to become a professional wrestler"). He has discovered his true self ("I was meant to be somebody else"), his inner stud ("rich, successful, and the recipient of more ass than a toilet seat"). He knows the road to success will be long and hard ("Don't think you gonna make a living doing this bullshit"). And though he is tested with doubts of faith ("I had no desire to be some five-hundred-dollar-a-week, throw-your-ass-around-the-ring, dress-me-up-in-a-clown-suit dipshit"), he perseveres, facing any challenge and enduring every hardship ("I've got to defy death occasionally"). Eventually, perhaps after losing his way ("So that was how I got into taking drugs"), he learns the most important lesson of all. He has to believe in himself ("If it's to be, it's up to me"). And with that, he comes into his glory ("I am an object of, of, of . . . of DESIRE!") and achieves the wisdom that only comes from experience ("Now I see it for what it was . . ."). The journey complete, he can now bestow wisdom on his fellow man ("what better training is there for public office?").

Separation, initiation, return: it is the classic monomyth that Joseph Campbell outlines in *The Hero with a Thousand Faces*, providing a kind of allegorical instruction for the transformative journey that a lot of young men hope to take. Maybe someday, Hawxhurst said, he would write his own biography—or at least get me to ghostwrite it for him. Meantime, the way he would tell his life story was simply to live it.

A FEW MONTHS after his Viking Hall debut, Hawxhurst invited me down to New Orleans, initially to introduce me to his wife. By the time I made it down to Louisiana, though, they weren't calling each other baby anymore. In fact, Hawxhurst was moving out. So instead of spending time with his son, we mostly just drove around town in his Dodge Ram, catching up with Oren's friends. The huge four-wheel-drive truck was obviously the one thing in his life he could take complete satisfaction in. "I'm the kind of person who makes sacrifices for what he wants," he said of the $450 monthly car payments, nearly half his paycheck.

"But why did you get such a big truck?" I asked.

"Because guys with big dicks drive big trucks."

"I would think it would be the opposite, like a bit of over-compensation."

He asked what kind of car I drove.

"I don't. See what I'm saying?"

Whenever I made a crack like that, Hawxhurst would say, "Dude, you are so gay!" But as we drove out to Jean Lafitte Swamp, where we spent an afternoon harassing a one-eyed, three-legged alligator, Hawxhurst admitted that my take on the truck was not completely wrong—in the emotional sense, that is. Talking about what an asshole his father was, he said: "Do I want to show him up? Fuck, yeah! *That's* why I bought this truck."

The truck and his father aside, the challenge Hawxhurst faced was this: How could he matter in this life? Along with that came a related question: How could he prove his worth as a man?

The self-doubts those questions raised seemed one reason he clung tenaciously to his conviction that wrestling was real.

"It's not like people who are into *Star Trek*," he said at one point. "Those people think it's real. They talk and think about it all the time. There's a big difference."

"How so?" I asked.

"Wrestling is real. We know *Star Trek* is not reality."

"But professional wrestling *isn't* real," I said. "Is it?"

"Yes, it is," he insisted. "It's more real than *Star Trek*. I'm talking about the people who watch *Star Trek* and make it their life. It's fine to watch it, but don't confuse it with real life."

As I say, Hawxhurst was only twenty, and he said a lot of things I didn't agree with. But all that week, I kept coming back to this, determined that he should accept my (to him) disparaging view of pro wrestling. And he wouldn't. Neither would his friends Mickey and Rashad, nor would the guy at Freaky Tiki Tattoos, who tattooed a naked Evelyn Nesbitt, the turn-of-the-century showgirl, on my right arm. None of them were wrestling fans, but they didn't see what the big deal was. "If Oren thinks it's real," Rashad said philosophically, "then to him it is."

"It's kind of like the difference between 'real' wrestlers and the 'joke' wrestlers," Hawxhurst added.

"I don't understand the difference," I said. "Hulk Hogan can't actually wrestle. Everybody knows that. So is he a 'joke' wrestler? I mean, all of you guys are entertainers."

"Exactly."

"But you're not athletes."

"Oh, I'm definitely an athlete," Hawxhurst said.

"But you're not competing," I said. "You're performing."

"I take that as a big insult. That's totally putting wrestling down. Let me ask you something—is monster trucks a sport?"

"I don't know."

"Answer the question. Is monster trucks a sport?"

I said that I had no idea, that I'd never seen a monster truck show, that I didn't know if they raced or just revved their engines or what. The athleticism of wrestling, to my mind, was analogous to ballet—rougher, cruder, louder, more violent, but it's still about people using their bodies to tell a story. "Plus," I said, "in wrestling there's this whole other element of fakery and exaggerating, which I think is great. It's what makes wrestling so fun. It's always who's bullshitting who. It's one layer of bullshit on top of another. But somewhere in there, there's a little bit of truth. And everybody is trying to figure out what that is."

"And the truth is," Hawxhurst said, "I'm an athlete and you're an asshole!"

F AIR ENOUGH. Obviously I had my own cultural prejudices, and they were getting in the way of taking Hawxhurst seriously. If he wanted to call himself an athlete, who was I to argue otherwise? Fortunately, by now we had become good friends. Whenever we met up at shows, the first thing he would do is give me a big bear hug. To be funny, he'd kiss my forehead. He'd call me Dawg or Dude or Daddy-o. "What up, fucker?" he'd say, leaving long rambling messages on my answering machine that sounded like he was drunk, though he seldom drank and never took drugs. It was like being friends with Eminem, without the attitude. He seemed to have hundreds of friends; they called each other incessantly on their cell phones, giving hourly progress reports on their day. "Dude, it was *so* funny!" is how every conversation came to an end. But then he'd hang up and a needy expression would come over his face that would break my heart. Kevin Lusignan, a high school guidance counselor, told me he couldn't begin to count the times Oren has cried on his shoulder. And when Hawxhurst called me, I often sensed him angling for consolation or guidance. But he didn't know how to ask for it and I didn't know how to offer it, so instead we talked about wrestling.

What was remarkable about the flamboyant histrionics of pro wrestling was the degree to which they resembled the coming-of-age rituals practiced elsewhere in the world. Wrestling—especially the bloody hardcore kind that Hawxhurst participated in—was even more brutal than critics maintained. A team of paramedics was always on hand for a reason; they were put to work at every show. While not exactly planned, the injuries weren't exactly mishaps, either. They were just a necessary and altogether expected part of the rite.

From the dawn of humanity, boys have undergone elaborate tests and trials, invariably involving bloodshed and the risk of injury, to prove their masculinity. Girls are seldom subjected to violent initiation rites. No matter how she might feel about her femininity, a teenage girl has little doubt that she is well on her way to becoming a woman; the onset of menstruation proves as much. Biology offers no similar marker for boys. Instead, manhood is culturally forced through ritual ordeal. In the less-than-comfy past, isolated tribal and frontier cultures needed able-bodied men to protect and provide. Elaborate initiation rites ensured that young men could meet those demands; they also effectively codified community val-

ues. Yet even in tamer times, when most young men found
work in jobs that the "weaker sex" performed equally well (if
not better), a boy's passage into manhood still seemed to require, in Norman Mailer's words, "small battles with honor."

The problem was that, since real-life battles rarely arise
anymore, a man must be something of an actor, putting on a
culturally scripted performance of masculinity. To be big and
tall helped, but a man also had to have a large spirit, as evi-
denced by his free spending and insatiable sexual appetite. For
the Mehinaku Indians, in central Brazil, these qualities come
into critical focus on the wrestling grounds, where men strut
and swagger in a routine scarcely different from the posturing
in WWE's *Raw*. For the Mehinaku, the conspicuous display of
an extravagant masculinity is but one stage in a process, not an

end in itself. Excessive violence, high emotions, quarreling, competitiveness, and a rather feminine flamboyance characterize this "liminal," or threshold, state. Initiates are allowed to think that they are the epitome of masculine beauty, virility, and valor. It is understood, though, that the narcissism is only temporary and transitional, since the ultimate social objective is to defeat childhood narcissism and reincorporate initiates in a new role as self-sacrificing adults, taking a more responsible role within the community.

For boys like Oren Hawxhurst, wrestling's exercises in suffering and self-promotion likewise held out the promise of transformation. In the so-called death matches, for example, nobody really dies (or, anyway, they're not supposed to); instead, the wrestler experiences a ritual death of a weaker lesser self in order to be reborn and redeemed as a stronger, tougher, more manly man.

It seemed, though, that since wrestlers continually subjected themselves to the same horrific abuse, the ritual didn't quite confer any lasting sense of manhood on its participants. They instead seemed stuck in that liminal state of primary narcissism, without any further objective. They didn't cease clowning for attention. And perhaps that was always the idea. Perhaps wrestling wasn't intended to help young men get over adolescent fixations. Perhaps the ritual, like the outcome of the matches, wasn't meant to have any social legitimacy. That way, fans and wrestlers would feel compelled to keep returning to the same regressive experience, never satisfied that the catharsis had been complete. Perhaps the whole of American popular and commercial culture was designed to keep everyone in an anxious state of adolescent inadequacy and uncertainty.

Anyway, the more I thought about it, the better I understood that the make-believe competition of wrestling was indeed "real" for Hawxhurst and millions of other young men—real in the sense that something real and important was at stake: their worth as men. And my saying that wrestling *wasn't* real was, to Hawxhurst, the same as saying that it, and therefore he and his concerns, didn't matter.

A T THE END of my visit, Hawxhurst and I would drive from New Orleans to a country crossroads in Cornelia, Georgia, east of Atlanta. There and back, it would be a twenty-four-hour, 1,100-mile trip. Not wanting to put the mileage on his truck, Hawxhurst mooched a ride from another wrestler named Matt Griffin and also invited his twenty-eight-year-old uncle Timmy along to help with the driving. Timmy was a long-distance trucker who was also extremely fond of black women, of all ages, of all shapes and sizes. There was not one, in Louisiana, Mississippi, Alabama, or Georgia, that Timmy didn't want to have sex with, and he made sure to tell us. In addition to women, we talked a lot about wrestling. Like what made Ric "Nature Boy" Flair so classic and how full of crap Hulk Hogan was and how if Oren could only get the kind of push that lunkheads like Bill Goldberg were getting, he'd be famous, too.

"I want to be on TV," Hawxhurst stated for the record. "Not just being in the background, waving like an idiot, but you know. . . . I'm attracted to things like that. Anything where I can be seen. Like, did you know that, on the computer, there's a guy in Belgium that's got pictures of me all over his website? To have someone that far away know who you are—that's awesome."

Griffin professed not to care about things like that. The fact that they would not be paid for their work that night didn't concern him. Neither, he claimed, did it matter to him that the show would be broadcast on cable access. A public relations flak for the Marines, and a few years older than Hawxhurst, Griffin was always going on about accepting obscurity and not chasing after unrealistic dreams.

"What? And end up working at McDonald's?" Hawxhurst said. "I ain't ever going to ask nobody if they want fries with that!"

"I look at it like, if you're a musician and only play small clubs, that doesn't mean you're not as good as someone with a top-forty hit," Griffin said. "It just means you have something else to offer."

"Meanwhile, Justin Timberlake is getting all the pussy."

Griffin affected a superior philosophical air, as if the prerogatives of pop singers were entirely irrelevant to the discussion. "I *would* like to have my own action figure," he finally allowed.

"Who wouldn't want to have his own action figure?" Hawxhurst snorted. "Anybody who tells you they don't is full of shit."

There was an uncharacteristic vehemence to this declaration that silenced everyone. For about a half hour we just drove along. Hawxhurst's thoughts drifted to that night's show, to the push that he hoped to get from the show's promoter, and whether it might lead to greater acclaim. Then he started thinking about how he intended to behave when he finally did make it big. Would he, for instance, throw some cash his father's way or give him squat? He didn't know what would be more satisfying. But he did know that, no matter how successful he became, he wouldn't change. He wouldn't get a big ego just because he was a famous wrestler, he told us. If a fan wanted to talk to him, he would always make time. "Because you don't know what he's going through, where he's coming from. For that five minutes of his life, he feels good about himself because you're talking to him. People need that."

# CHAPTER SIX

MY HEART YEARNED TO BE KNOWN AND LOVED.
—FRANKENSTEIN'S MONSTER
(FROM THE NOVEL BY MARY SHELLEY)

THE APPLICATION FORM to Roland Alexander's All-Pro Wrestling Boot Camp, located in an industrial section of Hayward, California, ends by asking prospective students to explain why they want to be professional wrestlers. They're supposed to answer in fifty words or less, and most applicants get right to the point:

BLAKE, 19: "I hope to have people looking up to me."

LOUIE, 20: "Because it has been a lifelong dream to have thousands of people chanting my name."

**JIM, 26**: "Basically I hear that you get laid a lot."

**ALLEN, 18**: "Because professional wrestlers are chick magnets."

**JONATHAN, 22**: "So I can make big bucks and be on TV."

**DAVID, 18**: "Because I get goose bumps watching the wrestlers do what they do."

**TAYLOR, 20**: "Because I believe everyone has a gift and that my gift is wrestling—I just need somewhere to showcase my talents."

**ELI, 23**: "Because there is a great person inside of me waiting to break out and this could be the opportunity for this breakout to happen."

**DAVID, 21**: "I want to win over a crowd with a persona not my own."

**SEAN, 19**: "I want to accomplish something big and change my life for the better."

**KEITH, 20**: "I have the body for it and a who-gives-a-fuck attitude."

**DARRYL, 17**: "I love the glory that comes upon wrestlers."

**DAMIEN, 17**: "Because my whole family has put me down."

**JUSTIN, 20**: "Because I got a big heart."

I don't think I met a single serious wrestling student who did not have an enormous heart. It was their defining characteristic. They were fat and skinny, short and tall, big and puny, tough and wimpy, but despite the odds, they all dared to find out if they had the stuff that dreams are made of. An older wrestler once told me: "In this business, it is liars lying to other liars. Basically, we're all lying fucks." They weren't, though, especially those toiling away while others traipsed off to the celebrity ball. They may have been full of starry-eyed delusions, but they had an ingenuousness that you could not help but admire. Many of the applicants to Alexander's school, feeling stumped, said they could not imagine doing anything else, that they were born to be wrestlers, that it was their destiny, that a divine force was leading them to this glory. And if they didn't have what it takes—well, that was okay, too. "Trying is a good thing," wrote Corey, age twenty-two.

Back in the days of regional territories, an eager novice would hang around an arena until some gruff old grappler decided to show him the ropes. That kind of thing just didn't happen anymore with either WWE or WCW. They were too big, too corporate. But, supply responding to demand, just about anybody who had ever worn a pair of spandex tights decided to open a wrestling school in the mid-1990s.

Alexander's was one of the first, though he himself was never wrestling material—a fact he didn't realize until he actually got in the ring. Short and spherical, he had stubby arms, skinny legs, and no chin to speak of. With dieting and exercise he might have improved his chances. But he hated dieting and exercise. In fact, what Alexander loved about wrestling wasn't even wrestling *per se*. He loved the milieu. He loved the con and the camaraderie of it. Just hanging around the locker rooms as a kid growing up in the Bay Area, running errands for wrestlers like Rocky Johnson, father of The Rock, he picked up "kayfabe," a language that old-school wrestlers learned from carneys that allowed them to discuss a work—a gimmick, a put-on, a performance—without fans understanding a word. The argot is a little like pig latin but more impenetrable. In fact, the entire world of professional wrestling was pretty forbidding. Even with their wives, wrestlers were expected to maintain the fiction that the fighting was real and the grudges sincere. At all times, and even in their own eyes, they were supposed to appear larger than life.

"At first I saw them as superheroes," Alexander told me. "But once I smartened up, I still loved the mystique of it—how the wrestlers maintained the secrecy, how difficult it was to be let in—and I was obsessed with penetrating that world."

J OHNNY RODZ, who runs a wrestling school out of Brooklyn's Gleason's boxing gym, where Mike Tyson and Roberto Duran (among many others) once trained, says that to be let in on the game "you have to get your face pushed into the mat, you have to pay your dues, you have to learn the fundamentals, the holds and take-downs. You can't just call yourself a professional wrestler. If it was that simple," he says, "every Tom, Dick, and Harry would be doing it."

But, actually, you *could* just call yourself a professional wrestler, and lately every Tom, Dick, and Harry *was* doing it. Alexander believed that learning "the art and science of wrestling" was a rewarding experience in and of itself, even if his students got no further than performing in front of a few friends and family members. Besides, it wasn't like his students were about to take up golf or tennis or outdoorsy sports like rock climbing or the pseudo-mysticism of yoga. Nor were they the types to audition for a production of Ibsen, although they did love performing. Wrestling was the medium where they could best express themselves.

A few years ago, Alexander considered applying for accreditation as a legitimate trade school. If you could go to a beauty school to study the mysteries of cosmetology—or, for that matter, if you could enroll in a graduate fine arts program to study the elements of acting or dance—why shouldn't wrestling be legitimized? What was the difference? What made yoga a more credible pursuit? He had trained and qualified instructors. He had a curriculum. He had "texts" (videotapes of classic matches and exemplary technical wrestlers). He had handouts. He had testing at the end of each semester. The lobby of the school resembled a doctor's waiting room, with brochures and information forms neatly fanned out on a console. The floors were carpeted and the walls painted baby blue, like a children's nursery. His instructors emphasized the fundamentals of straight amateur wrestling—holds, lockups, reversals, and takedowns—before turning to the nuances of performing and the meaning of wrestling's cultural tropes. They climbed into the ring one or two at a time, improvised a scene on a given theme (vengeance, perseverance, pride . . . ), after which instructors and fellow students offered their critique. What are you trying to say? they asked. What's the best way to say it? With a body slam? A clothesline? What's the underlying conflict of the drama? How do you reveal that? What allegiances are you invoking? What anxieties are you provoking?

Essentially, they were learning ways of articulating their experiences as young American men, and for many that alone satisfied a basic need. "Even if I don't make it to the WWE," writes Robert, a twenty-four-year-old fireman, "I'd be happy to perform in a room of a hundred people just to know for that fifteen minutes I told a story that they were glued to from beginning to end."

The person with the most compelling story to tell was Michael Thornton, age twenty-two. Born with a cleft palete, he also wore Coke-bottle glasses and hearing aids in both ears. He had only a couple of fingers on each hand and a couple of toes on each foot. He was also very skinny and had a speech impediment. Thornton wasn't deluded; he knew the odds of ever making money at wrestling, let alone getting a call to WWE, where most of the stars were presented as paragons of masculine majesty, were minuscule. But he loved wrestling, in part because it held the possibility of miraculous personal transformation. It had taken in giants and midgets and pinheaded circus freaks and turned them into stars. "When my mom passed away a few years ago, I started thinking about what I wanted to do in life," Thornton told me after taking his turn cutting a practice promo in Alexander's semipro class—a class he would not have been allowed into if he hadn't aced the prerequisite amateur course. "And I remembered when I was a kid that I had a school folder with Andre the Giant's picture on it, and it just kind of clicked, that if someone that outside the norm could make it big, then wrestling just might be a place for me, too."

Alexander frankly doubted there ever would be a place for Michael Thornton in professional wrestling. "I knew what people would say about me—that I was a scumbag who was just taking his money," he said. "But then I started thinking: 'Is that fair to Michael Thornton?' I went back and forth. And finally I decided he has as much right to try to become a wrestler as anyone. If WWE wants to shut him out, let WWE take the heat for that. But I'm not going to. He's pursing a dream, and that's what we're selling in this business—a dream. Most of these guys, they're couch potatoes who have done nothing but watch wrestling their entire lives. All of a sudden they get this idea in their head that they're going to pursue wrestling. They just can't wait to strut their stuff. They go to an indie show and see guys whose bodies aren't all that different than theirs. They say, 'If that guy can do it, I can do it, too.' They're ridiculously unrealistic, and most quit after a couple of weeks. But it might be the first real ambition they've ever had. I always tell them the absolute truth: 'The chances of your being a pro wrestler are slim to none.' But they want that ego satisfaction. They want to be able to walk down that aisle, hearing the fans screaming their name. It's a rush. To me, that's what indie wrestling is all about: decent human beings pursuing a dream. And you don't have to pay them a lot."

"If at all," I said.

"Exactly. If at all."

F I HAD wanted to, ridiculing the ambitions of Alexander's students would have been all too easy. Not for nothing did *Requiem for a Heavyweight* point to pro wrestling as a proud man's ultimate disgrace. In spite of its enormous popularity, wrestling still seemed the apotheosis of idiocy to a lot of people. And in a way, that was precisely the point of the spectacle—to lampoon the celebrity narcissism and macho vanity that it gleefully epitomized. But the boys who dreamed of "the glory that comes upon wrestlers" never seemed to realize this. To them, wrestling symbolized not silliness in the extreme but the height of personal success.

It wasn't that they were especially egotistical or misguided. Like everyone, they were just searching for a sense of their own significance. And taking their cues from a celebrity-obsessed society, they saw in professional wrestling the valida-

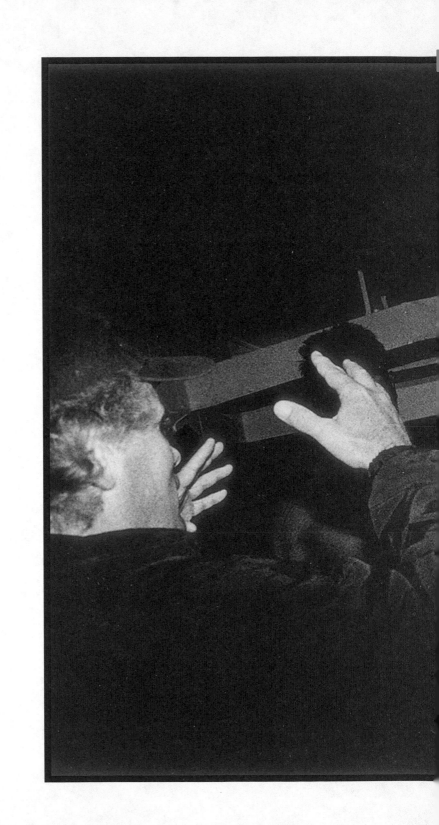

tion they craved. It gave them a feeling of camaraderie, of belonging to something bigger than themselves. Most importantly, it provided a forum for talking about being a young man in bewildering times. What was a man today? Was attention-getting meant to be a legitimate pursuit or a parody of achievement? Was it possible to accomplish something truly meaningful? Was everything just a performance, a stunt, a work, a gimmick in the service of personal vanity? Was being a buffoon better than being a nobody?

Few if any of them consciously asked those questions. They didn't need to. The questions were put to them implicitly, in every match of every show. The spectacle didn't necessarily resolve the conflicting messages they were getting about, say, success and masculinity, but it did dramatize those concerns. Shouting epithets, calling the performers fags and pussies, fans were able to directly address their anxieties. Wrestlers lived in that drama, however, and many simply lacked the wherewithal, and the self-worth, to recognize how their desperate need to be noticed might compromise their dignity, their masculinity, their self-esteem—the very things, that is, they hoped to gain by the experience. Like the insecure girl who makes herself available to any boy who pays her even debasing attention, they were just trying to feel valuable to somebody, anybody. And, naturally, an adolescent culture egged them on, telling them they were worth only as much as the attention they got—for what, it didn't matter.

The professional wrestler is, or at least plays, a supreme narcissist. Lacking a true sense of his self-worth and self-love, the narcissist invents a false self in a grandiose personal narrative. Becoming a kind of Frankenstein's monster, he usually manages to elicit some sort of response from others, which seems to confirm his importance. But when the world fails to validate his delusions, he feels exposed to feelings of inferiority and dependence. Small children are naturally narcissistic; their temper tantrums express their frustrations at learning they are not the center of the universe. Basically, the adult narcissist still hasn't come to grips with this painful fact. Unable to face the truth about himself, he lashes out at others and retreats further into his fantasies.

That professional wrestling dramatizes this psychology is obvious enough. That so many American boys would want to participate in that drama makes perfect sense. And that it should be so popular suggests that, far from being marginal to mainstream American experience, the psychology of pro wrestling is merely symptomatic of a narcissistic culture. In 1979, it was psychiatrist Christopher Lasch's diagnosis that America remained in this arrested stage of development. A decade that had produced primal scream therapy, nude workshops, touching exercises, assertiveness training, Rolfing, and something called "realistic therapy" (which required one to say "exactly what and who you are") offered ample proof of our inner childishness. An entire generation, observed Tom Wolfe, seemed hell-bent on "remaking, remodeling, elevating and polishing one's very Self, and observing, studying, and doting on . . . Me!" De Tocqueville noticed the tendency nearly 150 years earlier. "In democratic communities," he wrote, "each citizen is habitually engaged in the contemplation of a very puny subject, namely himself." To not be so engaged seemed almost a dereliction of one's duties as an American.

Of course, celebrities were still the exemplary Americans, figuring even more annoyingly in the public consciousness, but now the rest of us were enjoined to follow their narcissistic example. Witness business guru Tom Peters' advice to readers of the magazine *Fast Company*. "Ask yourself," he writes,

> what do I do that I am most proud of? What have I accomplished that I can unabashedly brag about? If you're going to be a brand, you've got to become relentlessly focused on what you do that adds value, that you're proud of, and most important, that you can shamelessly take credit for. When you've done that, sit down and ask yourself one more question to define your brand: What do I want to be famous for? That's right—famous for!
>
> I know this may sound like selfishness. But being CEO of Me Inc. requires you to act selfishly—to grow yourself, to promote yourself, to get the market to reward yourself.

That was in 1999, a year when professional wrestling's cult of egoism was once again striking a booming chord in the public imagination. Peters wasn't telling wrestlers anything they did not already know. He was just articulating the philosophy of professional wrestling for the rest of us.

W HY WOULD America embrace that philosophy? Why do spectacles of pathological narcissism flourish in the United States?

A liberal economist might argue that it's a function of consumer capitalism run amok—that is, of objectifying and commodifying human beings for the sole purpose of making money. Or maybe the "Me Inc." impulse was to be expected in a country with an expansive sense of democratic entitlement. Time was, one had to take enormous risk, demonstrate great courage, produce work of obvious value, reveal true originality, accumulate tremendous wealth, or wield awesome power to become widely known to strangers. To be an athlete, an actor, or an artist was rarely enough to achieve general fame outside one's profession. The ability to manufacture celebrity on a mass scale through the new communications technologies of the nineteenth and twentieth centuries radically changed all that—and changed, too, what we choose to admire. P. T. Barnum showed that you didn't have to be a great man to attract public attention. You could, in fact, be a very small man. The citizens of Bridgeport, Connecticut, had never been much impressed with a midget by the name of Charles Stratton. No matter, Barnum con-cluded: he simply "promoted" Stratton's rank in life. General Tom Thumb, as Stratton was now dubbed, "represented a new democratic midget," writes Leo Braudy in his history of fame, *The Frenzy of Renown*. The little general also represented a different kind of personage, one that "needn't have done—needn't do—anything special," as writer James Monaco sums up the new vocation of modern times, celebrity.

If the recent spate of reality-based television shows proves anything, it is that more of us than ever want in on the action. All that is required, it seems, is a willingness to drink liquefied pig's liver, to flop around in a vat of squid, to bob for chicken feet, to lie in a coffin full of rats, to eat sheep's eye-balls and reindeer testicles, to be tarred and feathered and force-fed worms, to reveal personal secrets, to put your pri-vate relationships up for public consumption, and to other-

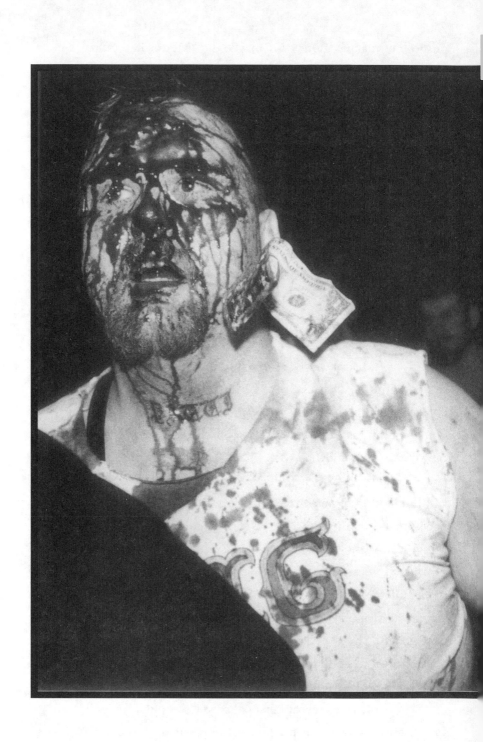

wise degrade yourself in whatever ways television producers can imagine.

One thing popular culture does is mediate the very disparities that it creates. Wrestling's young ingenues knew they weren't ever going to sit around exchanging scripted witticisms with the stars of *Friends* (to the tune of a million dollars per episode). But after ECW's hardcore revolution had turned misshapen miscreants like Mick Foley's Mankind into household names with bestselling memoirs to their credit, thousands of young men couldn't wait to enlist. They may not have had The Rock's awesome physique or Gorgeous George's gift for self-parody. What they had instead was a willingness to maim and mutilate their bodies and thereby achieve their own motley glamour. And the really cool thing was, you could start off doing it in your own backyard. You could jump off your parents' roof and light yourself on fire and suddenly find yourself known to boys all over the country—provided you videotaped the merriment and publicized it on the Internet. Like Johnny Knoxville and the guys on the TV show *Jackass*, the backyard wrestlers generally had a sense of humor about all the fabulously stupid stuff they did to themselves. Forming their own wrestling federation, giving themselves colorful wrestling names, staging shows and creating a website to honor their collective glory was partly an homage to, and partly a spoof on, big-time wrestling. It was also meant to burlesque a celebrity culture they desperately wanted to be a part of. "Videoing, being able to watch yourself—that was the whole point," Josh Piscura told me, explaining what got him started on his brilliant career as a backyard wrestler. "Then we started to get a reputation for doing crazy shit, and that was cool, too. It gives you an identity. You feel like a celebrity. You get noticed at the mall."

Shopping-mall fame must be something very special, because it turns out that boys all over the country suddenly had the same idea—that if WWE could manufacture synthetic celebrities, maybe they could do the same thing, just by "sticking a guy with a cattle prodder, bashing him with a crowbar, crashing through tables," as Bret Hart, a legendary wrestler of the old school complained. "Now it's all about hurting each other for stupid reasons."

HOWEVER that may be (I, for one, didn't think the reasons were completely stupid), Hart's criticism seemed to miss the point. Contrary to what most people said, wrestling was a very real competition—for attention. Whoever got the most, won. And won big; everyone else scrambled for the crumbs. It was as simple as that. For a time in the mid-1990s, for being what he described as "a radically cool guy," Hart enjoyed the lion's share. To win attention at the turn of the century, though, you hardly needed to enroll in an expensive wrestling school and follow in Hart's humorless footsteps. You were better off going to work for someone like Rob Zicari, president of Extreme Associates, as Billy Welch did before he was anointed wrestling's one and only Messiah.

"Here I have a chance to build myself up, to become a name, to achieve a status," The Messiah, a devout churchgoing Christian, said during a break from his work at Extreme.

"For all of us, something is missing," his colleague Ass-hole Andy Armageddon added. "We're compensating for things that are lacking in our lives. A certainty, a confidence, a feeling of power . . ."

"It's all a matter of developing a gimmick," The Messiah continued, not quite picking up on where Asshole Andy was going. "When I got my own T-shirt, I thought, 'That's it! I've made it. I can die now.' And now I go to the Northridge Mall and there are guys wearing it! It's fucking awesome! It's like being a movie star."

The two accommodating young men, both tall and blandly handsome in a Ben Affleck sort of way, had some fa-miliarity with movie stardom, of a sort. With offices deep in the semi-industrial heart of California's San Fernando Valley, Extreme Associates hoped to catch the recent wave of hard-core wrestling enthusiasm, launching its own brand of bed-lam. Unlike most other independent promotions, however, Extreme had experience in hardcore entertainment, produc-ing the raunchiest videos on the adult entertainment market. Its twenty-eight-year-old CEO reckoned the two businesses shared the same sleazy, white-trash demographic; and al-though there were billions to be made in porno, one thing it didn't really have was fans. It had consumers, yes. But they weren't buying porno action figures and porno bobblehead dolls. If somehow he could integrate the two industries . . .

Employees who had originally been drawn to work for Ex-treme Associates for the obvious reason—"to be around a lot of fucking"—had a joke for the company's new division. "Wrestling" they said, "is just another kind of love." Both, that is, constructed fantasies of power and pain. Both presented and *re*presented provocative "acts" for the pleasure of others. And there was no getting around it: both hardcore pornography and hardcore professional wrestling could be blatantly, brutally violent—at least the kind Extreme produced were. Asshole Andy Armageddon, a shy college English major whose real first name wasn't Asshole, or even Andy (it was Howard), had no interest in being on the receiving end of that violence. He was a porn star who, like a lot of actors, really wanted to direct. The Messiah, on the other, had worked as an all-purpose office lackey and was only interested in the sublime pleasure of his own pain.

"A death match is like jumping out of an airplane," The Messiah rhapsodized. "You've got beds of lightbulbs, beds of barbed wire, two beds of nails in each corner, and what's called the Supreme Bed of Gore, which is a regular bed with fluorescent lightbulbs—the long tubes—stacked like a pyramid with barbed wires wrapped around them. Before a match, I'm, like, 'Dude, suck it up and do it!' And it's awesome! It's hard to describe the feeling, but afterward you're like, 'I fuckin' did that!' "

"It's like your masculinity is on the line," Asshole Andy put in.

"Exactly!" says The Messiah. "My father, he always thought I was going to grow out of wrestling. Well, guess what? I'm not. He didn't raise no pussies, and a death match proves it."

And yet the weird thing was, the rites of professional wrestling, even the vile, filthy, bloody, and barbaric rites of the hardcore variety, also entailed a kind of feminine role-playing, subjecting young men to the tyranny of the so-called male gaze. As women were rejecting the role of mere objects of desire, men were embracing it. But embracing it anxiously— anxieties that pro wrestling addressed and, at least for some young men, helped resolve.

# CHAPTER SEVEN

---

YOU HAVE A PRODUCT AND THAT PRODUCT IS
YOURSELF.                    —DALE CARNEGIE

---

ORLD WRESTLING Entertainment made an important discovery in 1989. To avoid paying the New Jersey Athletic Commission a 10 percent fee on sports events, the company began calling the shows they produced "sports entertainment." Instead of compromising the business's credibility, as many feared, the candor did just the opposite, allowing fans to enjoy wrestling for what it obviously was: a purely theatrical performance—"a spectacle of excess," as French critic Roland Barthes called it.

I could understand why the frank acknowledgment of fakery upset fans like Joe Joe Russello. They knew that wrestling was completely bogus, but saying so seemed an end of innocence. Everything was an open sham now, and everyone knew it.

Everyone except the wrestlers, that is. In the past, they had always gone to great lengths to make "a work" (a performance) seem like "a shoot" (a real fight). Asked if wrestling was a sham, Gorgeous George said: "You might as well ask me if I beat my wife." The wrestler David Shultz had a more succinct response when *20/20*'s John Stossel called wrestling fake in a 1985 interview: he slapped the ABC reporter upside the head, proving exactly nothing. Amazingly, even though they were the ones telling the story, a lot of wrestlers clung to the belief that professional wrestling was a real sport and, therefore, they were real athletes. Joanie Laurer (Chyna) tells the story in her autobiography, *If They Only Knew*, of a veteran complaining to WWE scriptwriter Vince Russo about having to lose a match.

"I beat this guy!" the wrestler says. "I beat this guy!"

"Wait a minute," Russo shoots back. "You didn't beat anybody, okay. We wrote stories that had you winning— remember? Your win-loss record? That's fiction."

The awakening, as Laurer points out, could be rude—if they ever do wake up to reality. Many don't, and for the same reason that many wrestlers turn to drugs. They need the illusion of indomitable strength their fantasies give them.

The problem is, their illusions only open the way to new difficulties. Before they know it, their illusions become real; they become the egoists they played in the ring. Their commitment to self-exhibition effectively subverts the very gender roles they are trying to uphold.

In that, professional wrestlers are hardly alone. The sort of preening and primping that young men have to engage in to keep up their manly appearances plainly go against cherished archetypes of stoic American manhood. John Wayne's screen persona was the opposite of a showoff. Superman hid behind the guise of a mild-mannered reporter. The Lone Ranger wore a mask. Teddy Roosevelt aspired to the humble "self-contained" manner of the cowboy. Charles Lindbergh flew across the Atlantic, and spent the rest of his life flying away from fame. But somewhere between the humble and homely *Rocky I* and the amped-up *Rocky V*, the self-effacing stoicism of the mythic American man had gone by the boards. Where a man's identity had once derived from his actions, now image was everything. According to a recent Harvard University study, men today are even more preoccupied with their appearance than women. They are also more distressed by feelings of inadequacy. "Society is telling them now, more than ever before, that their bodies define who they are as men," write Harrison Pope, Katharine Phillips, and Roberto Olivardia in *The Adonis Complex*. The message to young men is relentless, they say—*You don't look good enough.*

Women have long been put in that position, and many of them have found it demeaning. "I wanted to be more than a gimmick," says Laurer, who at five-foot-ten, weighing 190 pounds, and bench-pressing more than 300 pounds, literally stood shoulder to shoulder with the men. "I didn't want to only be objectified." But men like her boyfriend at the time, the wrestler Hunter Hearst Helmsley, didn't seem to object.

Or maybe they did mind. Maybe the violence of professional wrestling was an expression of an inchoate resentment toward a society that reduced masculinity to mere image.

Maybe the narcissistic violence was meant to mask the fear they were really feeling. "The aggression is a mind-set you put yourself in," Asshole Andy Armageddon once explained. "It's psyching yourself up, because everybody knows that as soon as you stop being able to perform, you're worthless."

T HE THING IS, many men were able and willing to perform, if only someone would let them. Dropped by the bigger promotions, guys who had once enjoyed a degree of fame had to hustle themselves for anybody that would have them. They could usually find work, they just didn't always get paid. A wrestler-for-hire tried to make up for the lousy pay by selling his T-shirts and action figures on the indie circuit. "Just me and you, Buddy," he'd plead, offering to let you take his picture for the bargain price of five dollars.

"To *take* your picture? Not just to buy one?" I once asked the wrestler Little Guido, seeing that he was also selling eight-by-ten glossies of himself at three bucks apiece.

"Do you work for free?" he shot back.

"But this isn't work—it's getting your picture taken."

"It's merchandizing," he said.

I guess I was getting fed up with all of the pomposity of pro wrestling. I pointed out that Little Guido's action-figure doll did not even look like him.

"Oh, it's definitely me," he said.

"But how can you tell?"

"It's got a beard."

"But *you* don't have a beard," I said.

"It's me—I guarantee you."

A few weeks later I called Little Guido, whose real name was James Maritato. Not mentioning the earlier photo incident, I asked to tag along to another show on Long Island. Maritato had no affiliation with the company; he wasn't even sure of its name: Something Something Wrestling. Whatever. . . . In the independents, you show up; they tell you who you're working with, who wins, what the angle is, and, if you are lucky, you get paid a couple of hundred bucks, travel expenses not included.

It was not the sort of career Maritato had envisioned for himself. Beginning his apprenticeship after high school at a wrestling school in New Jersey, he'd always imagined that if he applied himself to learning a trade and paid his dues, working his way up in the guild, he'd eventually land a secure position with a reputable company. The heroic artisan, the honest worker who made his living by the sweat of his brow: that was the image he would cultivate. He began calling himself Precious Damien Stone, then switched to James Stone, then Gem Stone; when he formed a tag team known as the Full-blooded Italians (or FBI), he played his ethnic card, calling himself Little Guido. He had the right idea, as Italian-Americans have long been fiercely devoted fans of wrestlers like Bruno Sammartino and Antonino Rocco. Maritato was small, though, only five-foot-eight, and that had limited his prospects. There were exceptions, such as the great Mexican luchadors, famed for their masks and high-flying acrobatics, but smaller wrestlers with name-brand recognition were rare. He had another disadvantage. In a business chock-full of grade-A jerks, he wasn't one of them, I discovered. By his own description, he was a stereotypical blue-collar guy who happened to get snagged on the barbed wires of celebrity.

"All I'm looking for is that one chance," he said as we made our way from Tarrytown, north of New York City, into darkest Long Island. "I've been doing this for eleven years. I started off doing shoot wrestling. Nothing hardcore. No acrobatics. No body slams or hip-tosses. No bouncing off ropes. Just old-school stuff, unscripted, trying to make the other guy submit. That was pretty cool. I was twenty-two. I was working as a professional. I had arrived. I was on TV. People knew who I was. But then . . ."

But then the brave new economy collapsed.

For a few exuberant years, its cheerleaders had been breathlessly touting the freedom, flexibility, and self-affirming benefits that came to those who rejected the "old social contract." Citizens of what *Fast Company* called "Free Agent Nation" would no longer have to "submerge" their identity to a company. In this economy, "everyone is a star."

Not surprisingly, professional wrestling's recent renaissance coincided with such hubris. Wrestlers were its poster boys. None expressed the ideal of heroic individualism better than a beefy blond named Steve Williams. Beefy blonds being a dime a dozen in wrestling, Vince McMahon had not thought much of Williams when he first brought him into WWE. He called him The Ringmaster. But Williams had a platonic conception of himself as a shit-kicking Texas redneck who liked to drink beer, shoot guns, and drive needlessly large trucks. Reborn as Steve Austin—a name taken from the 1970s bionically enhanced character played by Lee Majors in *The Six Million Dollar Man*—Williams's regeneration as the ultimate *isolato* followed the archetypal American myth to the letter. The trucks, the boots, the leather vests, the jeans all invoked the ethos of the outlaw frontier, where real men were defiantly autonomous and free. True, it was a fanciful self-image for a man who played dress-up. However, the image worked—rather spectacularly, especially after "Stone Cold" Steve Austin coined a catchphrase that was a play on the rebirth theme. Austin had been waging a rivalry with Jake "The Snake" Roberts, a onetime crack addict who had been using the biblical reference John 3:16 (". . . .whosoever believeth in him shall not perish but have everlasting life") during a comeback attempt as a born-again Christian. Pinning Roberts in the final match of the June 1996 "King of the Ring" pay-per-view, the born-again badass Stone Cold Steve Austin exulted in his own conversion experience. Enough of John 3:16, he bellowed. "Austin 3:16 says I just whipped your ass!"

Of all the bombastic things wrestlers had always been saying, what made this catchphrase so unusually catchy is one of those elusive mysteries of marketing and mass psychology that every brand manager would dearly love to solve. For five long years Williams had been a no-name ham-'n-egger, bouncing from company to company, failing to build up any kind of fan following. Turns out, that experience would have a lot to do with his appeal. With frustrations of their own, fans could relate to Stone Cold becoming his own man. Which, obviously, he hadn't. Not really. He was simply playing a part McMahon and his scriptwriters had given him.

There were, however, thousands of others who really were fending for themselves. They had no choice in the matter. "Why I don't have a regular job somewhere—I don't have the answer," Maritato said. "I've always been dedicated and loyal. I'm a good worker. In ten years, I have only missed one

show, and that's because I drove and drove and couldn't find the damn place. Otherwise, I went in there every night and gave it one hundred percent, if not more. But I've learned that it's not how good you are. It's all about getting a break. There are thousands of wrestlers. But they can only hire so many, which means there are all these guys who deserve jobs and are just sitting around, waiting to get noticed."

I think it is this feeling of "deserving" that has vexed so many young men (and not just pro wrestlers) in Maritato's position. Despite the obvious chicanery, they still sort of believed in wrestling's conceit of every-man-for-himself fair play. If you worked hard and paid your dues, success would come. Wrestling advanced the spurious myths of laissez-faire capitalism at the same time that it exposed them. The world only pretended to be fair, wrestling said. In fact, it favored certain interests, just as it always had. It had rules and referees, but only the schmucks paid attention to them. The wrestler who had gotten over could tell himself—as all celebrities, indeed all really successful people, undoubtedly do—that his good fortune was the reward of a just meritocracy. But Maritato had discovered long ago that, in wrestling anyway, "deserving" had absolutely nothing to do with success of this kind, and neither did cherished notions of manliness; that success like Stone Cold Steve Austin's was all a matter of finding a marketable image of masculinity.

So until they found that image, workers like Maritato did what they had to—working for iffy outfits like Rob Zicari's Xtreme Professional Wrestling, for example.

ICARI and XPW first came to my attention during an Extreme Championship Wrestling show at the Olympic Auditorium, in downtown Los Angeles, where Classie Freddie Blassie and Superstar Billy Graham had reigned in the 1960s and '70s. I was sitting in the upper balcony, far from the madding crowds, and the show was doing absolutely nothing for me. But then one of Zicari's employees sitting in the front row—a porn star named Kristy Mist—created a small commotion by taking off her shirt and thus stealing the spotlight from one of the ECW babes. To me, the cheek of it came as a welcome provocation to what was becoming a tired ritual of chair shots and broken tables. I especially enjoyed the bunkhouse brawl that broke out when the entire ECW roster rushed from backstage, whaling on a posse of Zicari's wrestlers seated with Kristy.

"It was our way of saying, 'Fuck you! You're in our town,'" said Zicari, who wisely stayed home but nevertheless challenged Paul Heyman to a shoot—a real fight. "I'll kick his faggot ass all across Los Angeles."

By all appearances, Zicari is exactly the sort of sleazeball most people associate with porn—the sort that other pornographers like to pretend they aren't. He was on the phone, his feet kicked up on his desk, when I first dropped by the warehouse-cum-office in Van Nuys, the Hollywood of the adult entertainment industry, from which he managed both Extreme Associates, a porno concern, and its wrestling offshoot, XPW. "I don't give a fuck! This is what we fucking do!" he was screaming. "If she doesn't want to get slapped around, then fuck her—she's fired!"

Except for the mammoth desk, I wouldn't have guessed that I was looking at the owner of $10-million-a-year business, with twenty full-time employees. His ears, nose, and eyebrows thoroughly pierced, his goatee and muttonchops gone scraggly, his long hair dyed purple and clumped into dreadlocks, Zicari seemed just another Gen-X dude searching for his sense of individuality. Chewing an enormous wad of tobacco, he had filled dozens of Evian bottles with brown spit. They and a lot of whimsical doodads littered his desk. On the wall behind him was an autographed picture of somebody's scrotum. As he stood up to slam the phone down with extra force—"fucking cocksucker!"—I saw that, even with the five-inch rubber soles on his boots, he was not in the least physically forbidding.

"We're a fucking team," Zicari began telling a burly director obviously accustomed to the rants. "We've got running backs, wide receivers, and linemen, and we need everybody to do his job. At the end of the month, when I need to make payroll, and the gay movie makes four thousand dollars, and the she-male makes five thousand, and the bondage makes six, and the wrestling makes whatever, I'm able to sit here and go, 'Oh, wow, it looks like we'll all get paid.' "

Suddenly Zicari remembered something. "Oh, shit! I left my mom on hold. . . . Mom, are you there?"

"_____"

"Mom, Mom, Mom, listen—this is weird fucking shit. You just met this lady! She's going to think you're the most fucked-up person in the world. You *cannot* give her *Planet of the Gapes*."

He put the phone down, gently this time, and explained: his mom, a nurse, had mentioned to a patient that her son was a porno producer, and now she wanted to prove it.

Apropos of I wasn't sure what, Zicari hit on a new theme.

"I'm like fucking Martin Luther King!" he bellowed. "I get shot and killed so all you motherfuckers can have the freedom to be extreme!"

Despite the bluster, I quickly grew to like Zicari (even though he didn't take my suggestion for a classy PBS-style line of porno, called *Masturbation Theater*). I liked his candor and loved reading his scabrous yet sunny business updates on the Internet. A normal conversation was virtually impossible, however. In the middle of a thought, he would scream harmless obscenities at whoever came to mind. Esprit de corps being a constant theme of his orations, he liked to think that he was creating the atmosphere of a repertory company, something like the first years of *Saturday Night Live.* The aspiration appealed to his staff. They hadn't gone looking for a sense of community, nor did the culture tell them teamwork was a prescription for personal success, but that's what they found in companies like ECW and XPW, and they liked it. They were part of something. What they forsook in respectability they made up for in opportunity. You could start off answering phones at Extreme and in no time find yourself directing a film of your own. Meantime, the high quantity and low quality of the productions offered plenty of cameo work, if you were interested.

Kevin Kleinrock, Zicari's aide-de-camp, wasn't in the least. Like a lot of wrestling people I talked to, Kleinrock remembered exactly when destiny revealed itself: March 24, 1991, the night of WrestleMania VII. The son of a high school principal, he immediately began poring over eight wrestling magazines a month. In the back of one, he saw an ad for a book by one Percy Pringle. "So," the ad said, "you want to be a professional wrestler?" Actually, Kleinrock didn't. A proverbial ninety-eight-pound nebbish today, he was even gawkier in junior high. But he liked the idea of putting on a show, and promptly ordered Mr. Pringle's book, which mentioned a certain Slammers Wrestling Gym, in nearby Studio City. Fourteen years old when his parents took him to his first Slammers show, Kleinrock sounded just like Urial Yakobov describing his first live wrestling encounter: "I was immediately in love," he told me. "It was like, 'Oh, my God! I have to do this!' " And before he knew it, he was. While presiding over his high school speech and debate team and acting in productions of Shakespeare and Neil Simon, Kleinrock also worked for the makeup artist/country musician who owned Slammers. Attending UCLA, he majored in business, pledged a fraternity, became its president, got excellent grades, applied and got accepted to prestigious law schools. By then he had grown wiser to the ways of the wrestling business. Reading all those fan magazines, he noticed that night after night, even the big promotions were putting on essentially the same show. That impressed him. "I was confronted with the fact that everything, not just some of it, was undeniably, no doubt about it, a work. And I thought, 'How cool is that?' "

After his Slammers apprenticeship, Kleinrock got a call from Zicari, who'd been impressed by all the money that Vince McMahon was making and wanted some of it for himself. Kleinrock was given some fancy-sounding all-purpose corporate title that supposedly allowed him to concentrate exclusively on wrestling. As it turns out, the divisions at Extreme were not so neat. For instance: Kleinrock's office was also known as "the blowjob room," and this was not a figure of speech. Kleinrock didn't mind, though. In spite of eighteen-hour days, seven days a week, for six years running, what made working for a company with a lot of eager exhibitionists at his disposal so wonderfully worth it was the chance it gave him to live out fantasies of the nonsexual variety. "It's like having imaginary friends, except they're real," he said of his becoming a wrestling promoter before his twenty-first birthday. "Or like having a puppet show, except I have eight hands and I can do whatever I want with them."

I T WAS a much different story for the puppets. Promoters have always jerked wrestlers around, flinging them all over the country, bashing them about in every conceivable way, and in the end leaving them in a mangled heap of broken bones and broken dreams. That is the nature of a business where human beings are treated as disposable commodities. Whether the promoters were to blame for what Roddy Piper calls "the sickness" or the despair was to be expected in a profession that indulged delusions of full-blown narcissists, of the dozens of deaths in recent years, only a few had come as a surprise. Strung-out zombies who could only occasionally rouse themselves from a drug-addicted stupor to make noise about a comeback, these men already seemed to belong to the walking dead. If only for the name recognition, the rinky-dink independents might still hire them, no matter how difficult they were to work with. But the lousy pay and ignominy of performing for a few hundred fans when, not so long ago, they had strutted their stuff before hundreds of thousands, making upward of $20,000 for fifteen minutes' work at a pay-per-view, was more than many fragile egos could handle. Most killed themselves slowly, quietly, with Percocets,

Percodans, quaaludes, somas, morphine, cocaine, Oxycontin—you name it, they took it, until one night they took a few too many pills and, with the added stress of having spent years abusing anabolic steroids, died of a heart attack in some cutrate roadside motel.

The world of porn wasn't pretty, either, of course. Men in the business could tell themselves they were defending the last bastion of masculinity ("The one thing a woman cannot do is ejaculate in the face of her partner," one porn producer said. "We have that power"). The fact was, though, very few actors had the clout or made the money that the top actresses did, and inevitably that led to a lot of antifeminist frustrations. "You're just a hard dick—and sometimes you're not even that," an actor told me. The guys I met knew going in that nobody particularly cared about them; they weren't happy about it, but that was the reality of the business, and they accepted it. Wrestlers, on the other hand, never stopped hoping for praise and approval—a longing that went a long way toward explaining why so many careers ended in sorrow and early disorder.

"I can tell you," Rob Zicari said during a rare reflective moment, "wrestling is definitely an uglier business than porno. There are a lot more deaths, a lot more drug overdoses. There's this desperation to make it, and it takes its toll, mentally and physically. Before WWE took over everything, you could make thirty thousand bucks a year and feel satisfied that you had a good life. Now if you're not big enough or not strong enough or not 'over' enough, then you're fucked. You ain't going to wrestle. You ain't going to work. It's all or nothing."

HAD FLOWN out to Los Angeles specifically to see one of XPW's highly publicized "exploding death matches." But when I got there, Zicari and Kleinrock still did not have an arena to explode their wrestlers in. They apologized, saying that I was welcome to interview some of the company's wrestlers and valets, who would be working in their other capacity, on a porn shoot at a rented house in Malibu. "You probably don't want to do that, though," Kleinrock said. "It's really boring."

The author Susan Faludi would give me the same warning. I had recently read her book *Stiffed: The Betrayal of the American Man,* which sought to understand why men were struggling to find their footing in the 1990s. Not surprisingly, it was her chapter on the porn industry that most titillated reviewers. In her view, though, the difficulties of men in adult entertainment were merely symbolic of worries that men from all walks of life were suffering. Psychologically and otherwise, men everywhere were having trouble getting it up in a culture where what seemed to matter most was, as she writes, "mastering the art of self-presentation, fathering your own image, reproducing a self that could be launched into a mediated existence."

A couple days later, when I drove out to Malibu, I got a pretty good sense of what she was talking about. In an otherwise unfurnished living room, two men and an actress, all unclothed, sat on a poofy blue leather coach. As they were between takes, the actress was talking on her cell phone and the men were working individually on their erections, casually, while chatting with the crew. The other cast members sat around eating Doritos, bored goofy, waiting to shoot their scenes. A couple of actresses, like girls in church, failed to stifle giggles. One of them told me she was dying to pee but had to save it for her scene. Given the downtime, I thought I should introduce myself to the guys on the couch, not expecting that we would shake hands.

"Is this looking stupid or what?" one of the men asked.

"Stupid?" I said. "No."

"Really?"

"Really!"

Sitting there for the next several hours while the actors struggled mightily to "get wood," it occurred to me that I might as well have been watching wrestling. It was not just that wrestling dramatized sadomasochistic sexual rituals, or that the perverse scenarios seemed determined by unconscious wishes and fears, or that the role-playing appealed to patently prurient interests—those parallels to porn seemed obvious enough. What struck me was the way both were gripped by powerful male performance anxieties. If you could not perform, they both seemed to say, you weren't much of a man.

"This is the age of performance," Asshole Andy Armageddon would explain. "It's all about the art of the show."

"You're talking porn?" I clarified.

"Actually, I was referring to wrestling. But it's basically the same. It's about putting a performance over. Nothing else matters."

# CHAPTER EIGHT

I AM MY OWN COMMODITY.

—ELIZABETH TAYLOR

HEN OSCAR WILDE joked over a century ago that "the first duty in life is to assume a pose," he was expressing a subversive attitude—the philosophy of the dandy who could not be bothered with anything resembling real work. "What the second duty is," Wilde added, "no one has yet discovered."

Every age has had men who conspicuously reject the demands of traditional manhood. Until recently, though, they have belonged to a tiny elite, their defiance of conventions indicating superior social status. Today that dynamic has been turned inside out. Preening young men are searching for

status, not indulging a status they already enjoy. They are trying to flaunt their manliness, not flout it. For professional
wrestlers, that impulse creates some puzzling paradoxes. They
like to believe they have discovered their lost powers as men.
They call themselves "workers," for example, posing in jeans,
T-shirts, and construction boots; however, they aren't trying
to build anything, except their own celebrity. To not have a
regular job is a point of pride for even unknown wrestlers.
Lifting weights, tanning, fussing over their looks, living off
their forbearing mothers and wives and girlfriends, they
dream of the day when they will be lavishly admired for nothing but their appearance, objects of confused desire. Dandies
of the new millennium, they are in the business of making
spectacles of themselves.

Few of the rank-and-file wrestlers think about their quest
in just that way. Despite wearing makeup and performing
flamboyant skits, they still want to believe they are earning
their props as men.

The dandy is cousin to the drag queen, and in effect that
is what wrestlers are: men playing at being men, playing the
diva. Stereotypically, a drag queen is a transvestite, and more
than a few wrestlers have played that role, or something close
to it. Even extravagantly macho wrestlers like Jesse Ventura
borrowed the favorite accessory of femme flamboyance, the
feather boa. In his own way, Hulk Hogan was as over-the-top
as RuPaul. After shaving what looked like extraterrestrial crop
patterns in his chest hair early in his career, he then discovered
depilatory cream, baby oil, steroids, and intensive tanning.
Hunter Hearst Helmsley seemed to have modeled himself on

OPPOSITE: KING KONG BUNDY

Tom of Finland's gay erotica. Steve Austin looked to be auditioning for the Village People.

"Over," a term of high praise in wrestling (as in, "Dude, you are so over right now!"), came directly from the world of drag (only there the word was pronounced *ovah*), and it had the same meaning—not that you were done, finished, yesterday's news, but that you had succeeded in making yourself legendary, the center of attention, the belle of the ball. Sex and gender were almost beside the point. It was more about the experience of adulation. "I want people to notice me and look at me really closely," a performer named Lola tells writer Holly Brubach in *Girlfriend: Men, Women, and Drag*, adding that, though he dresses as one, he is not particularly interested in being or even looking like a woman. "I just want to be looked at, that's all."

So do professional wrestlers. Their entrances from backstage ape the "voguing" on the runway at a fashion show or drag ball. They stop, pivot, pose, and proceed down the long ramp toward the ring with an air of unflappable glamour. Where fashion models and traditional drag queens are playing on conventions of female beauty, wrestlers are invoking the clichés of masculinity, trying to create an illusion of an idealized manhood. Ironically, that required an effeminate attention to image and display. Even the wrestlers who seemed to defy glamour, the hairy and hideous ones with missing teeth and razored foreheads, were committed to the art of extravagant vanity, inviting fans to bask in their radiance.

S o WHY would so many avowedly "manly" young men embrace a patently antimasculine philosophy? Looking for an answer, I wanted to meet the one wrestler since Gorgeous George who seemed to grasp the dichotomy. Dwayne Johnson was his name.

Once a *USA Today* high school all-American, Johnson had seen his dreams of football glory fizzle out at the University of Miami, where he played second-string to two future all-pro defensive linemen. Passed over by the National Football League, he found himself in Canada, on the practice squad of the Calgary Stampeders. A couple of months later, the Stampeders decided Dwayne was not even worth the $175 they were paying him each week. Despite all the preaching about persevering in the face of adversity, Johnson was beginning to understand that an athlete was just "a piece of meat. And if you can't play, you're just a piece of shit."

Feeling rejected and quite literally worthless (as an athlete, anyway), Johnson's call to adventure began, as they usually do, in a moment of personal crisis. "My football career was over. There was nowhere else to go," he said, thinking perhaps he should get a regular job and come to terms with humdrum reality. But after flying from Calgary to his home in Miami, he had a sudden epiphany. Late that night, from a convenience-store pay phone, he called his parents. He needed his father to come get him.

"I was twenty-three years old and standing in a phone booth in the dead of night. I had no money, no car, no job prospects," he recalls. "I needed my dad's help. *Immediately.*"

He wanted his father to train him as a professional wrestler. His father was dead-set against it. He'd been a champion in every territory in the country, only to find himself making a measly hundred dollars a night at the end of his career, getting thrown around by punk kids half his age. That was if he got hired. Most weekends he didn't, and either went on drunken benders or stayed in bed, sleeping off yet another hangover, slowly doing what other wrestlers had done more swiftly with a bullet to the head. "One day we crave for mere subsistence, and the next we stand on the pedestal!" Jim Londos once said. But that, Johnson had learned, was only half the story. "One day you're getting the adulation of the crowd, the next you're broke," he says. "You're standing there at the bus stop and guys are coming up to you, saying, 'Weren't you Rocky Johnson?' "

In a scenario pregnant with oedipal drama, father and son argued for a week before finally stepping into the ring. "We leaned into each other, a very aggressive intergenerational lockup, as if we each had something to prove, which I guess we did," Johnson says. "I bore in on my father, went right to town on him, kicking him in the gut, pushing him into the corner, nailing him with one punch after another . . . reveling in the viciousness of it all, not even giving him a chance to breathe." And by the end of the workout, he realized: *This is me—a violent son of a bitch!*

A violent son of a bitch with an eye for image; for no sooner had Johnson won over his father than he began thinking about a look, a name, a gimmick. He says he didn't want to ride anyone's coattails, and at first resisted his mother's suggestion that he call himself Rocky Maivia, a combination of his father's first name and his Samoan grandfather's last. "I wanted to be known as the real deal, not some half-ass cartoon character," Johnson said. Exactly what it meant to be "the real deal" in a make-believe world was complicated, however. Johnson was not out to prove that he was a genuine professional athlete; he had already tried to do that and failed. Nor was he trying to prove that he could take and give a beating. Years of high school and college football had laid those insecurities to rest, if he ever had them. He wanted, rather, to be loved and admired simply for the person he was.

For his first match, a tryout for WWE in Corpus Christi (which he never would have had without his father's connections), Johnson borrowed a pair of white boots his dad had used in the 1970s. He shaved his hair short on the sides, long on top, making his head look like a pineapple. He still didn't have a gimmick, though. "What are we calling you, anyway?" asked Bruce Pritchard, who directed the "gorilla position," the area just behind the black curtain through which the performers make their grand entrances, named after the wrestler Gorilla Monsoon who, late in life, worked as a kind of stage manager of WWE.

"Dwayne Johnson."

"Dwayne Johnson? That's it?"

"That's it."

"Okay. Dwayne Johnson it is."

Thus began the brilliant career of a wrestler who would soon thereafter become known to millions of people around the world as The Rock.


ASTA LA VISTA, Ah-nuld!" Hollywood pronounced five years later in advance of Johnson's star turn as a screen actor. "When *The Scorpion King* opens, the reign of a certain fifty-something movie superhero will be all but terminated."

That wasn't how it worked out exactly (in California, politics gives fading movie stars another place to perform), but the comparison to Arnold Schwarzenegger was exactly right. As professional posers, both men had brilliantly managed to recast their foppish preoccupation with appearance as the quintessence of butch masculinity. They invited young men to gaze longingly at their bodies, yet somehow reassured them that, in doing so, they were fortifying themselves against any effeminate tendencies. Each, too, epitomized the "new kind of eminence" that historian Daniel Boorstin identified forty years earlier in *The Image*, a landmark of cultural criticism:

> He is the human pseudo-event. He has been fabricated on purpose to satisfy our exaggerated expectations of human greatness. . . . He is made by all of us who willingly read about him, who like to see him on television, who buy recordings of his voice, and talk about him to our friends. His relation to morality and even to reality is highly ambiguous.

By contrast, a "real" athlete has to prove in a rule-bound contest that he is superior to his competition. No matter how cleverly he has been branded and marketed, come Sunday afternoon Tiger Woods, working alone, has to finish four rounds of golf with a lower aggregate score than anyone else; otherwise he loses. His value as a brand ultimately depends on hard proof of excellence. There was something kind of premodern about the ethic, though. As brand manager of Me Inc., Johnson understood what his football coaches obviously didn't, stuck as they were in quaint industrial-era theories of labor value. Even if professional football teams had no use for his body, Johnson knew that it still had tremendous value as a fetish object, in both Freud's and Marx's use of the term. Millions of people could be persuaded that this commodity called The Rock, sold to them in the form of action figures, T-shirts, or as an image on TV and in movie theaters, might add some ineffable value to their lives. His iconography created the illusion of significance independent of reality. That was what made the gimmick he finally arrived at (calling himself The

Rock, speaking in the third person) so inspired. Dwayne Johnson the person had been eliminated from the equation, leaving only the commodity, the instantly recognizable product, like a can of Coca-Cola, something that would have a life of its own, separate from the person it was born of.

All of which made me wonder, as I waited to meet Johnson in the swank Jean Georges restaurant in the Trump International Hotel overlooking Central Park: What to call him? In the back of some dictionaries, they tell you how to address a king, a queen, a pope, or a maharajah, should the occasion arise. But what do you call a simulacrum, a human pseudo-event? Was it *Mr.* Rock? Or just plain Rock? Or maybe he went by his first name, The?

I really didn't know. Nor did I know how awed I was supposed to be. Johnson was clearly on his way to becoming a marquee star, and my instinct was to be duly impressed by that. Why, though? What had Johnson done exactly? He'd put a performance over and launched himself into a mediated existence. He'd become a name, literally. For that, I didn't believe he was any worthier of my admiration than Oren Hawxhurst or James Maritato. Or, anyway, that's what I told myself. The fact is, celebrity of Johnson's magnitude has an undeniable gravitational effect, warping one's better judgment. Once someone reached a certain level of visibility, what he'd done to achieve that notoriety hardly mattered. It was the image culture's version of Descartes's well-known supposition: "Someone (it doesn't matter who, it doesn't matter why) thinks I'm famous, therefore I am famous." But not only that: you were also, by mere virtue of that popularity, thought to be important, a figure of indisputable prestige. Thus, my merely mentioning that I would be interviewing The Rock more than impressed friends of mine who weren't wrestling fans; it somehow validated *me* in their eyes. I was writing about a famous person, so I must be doing something important.

Sitting near me in the restaurant were five players on the Orlando Magic basketball team, including their injured star, Grant Hill. As Johnson entered the room joined by two bodyguards, his agent, the movie's publicist, and the woman who kept him "looking tight"—his stylist—the basketball players suddenly snapped to attention. Real athletes cowed by a pretend athlete, even they were impressed, giving The Rock bashful nods of hello and nodding respectfully my way, too, as Johnson and I introduced ourselves.

I decided to go with Dwayne.

J OHNSON'S ENTOURAGE sat at another table, giving us our space. After the initial pleasantries, he ordered a gargantuan breakfast: egg-white omelette made with eight eggs and American cheese, grilled chicken, toast, fruit salad, a sliced tomato, and four large pancakes. When the waiter brought only three plate-sized pancakes, Johnson sent the meal back.

"When you ask for four, you expect four," he said.

We began by talking about the $60-million action-adventure movie he was starring in. What really interested me, though, was how Johnson felt about being a fetish object—not the easiest subject to broach with someone that you have just met, especially someone twice your size. Johnson was surprisingly game, though. "This is interesting," he said as I tested the waters with questions couched in a discussion of his acting. "I like thinking about these things." And I was glad he did, but already the aura was fading. Sitting next to me, he wasn't an icon. He was just a guy talking about his job. And what that came down to, he said, was "fulfilling your expectations." That's what his role both at WWE and in movies were about, he said—"delivering the goods." The person who plays an icon "shouldn't be butt-ass ugly." And in that regard, he added, "I have been very fortunate: people like to look at me. It's an image thing. In sports, it's different. You either do the job or you don't. It's not about image. That was appealing to me."

"But there you failed," I pointed out. "You got cut."

"I guess you're right," he said, chewing on the matter. "You know those wrestlers who haven't made it, who never will make it, who are still hoping that somehow they will? I was that guy. There's a quote in my book [*The Rock Says*], from Shakespeare: 'Some are born great, some achieve greatness, some have greatness thrust upon them.' I had that written down on my fridge, where every morning for five years I would look at it. I don't know why, but it meant a lot to me. You would like to think that as human beings we have a fair amount of control of our destiny, that making congruent decisions on a daily basis is going to lead you where you want to go. But then things get shifty. Sometimes we don't have as much control as we think we do. Others have the control, and it's difficult. I was always thinking, 'Okay, I'm going to outwork everybody else. My patience and perseverance is going to lead me where I want to go.' But it didn't work out that way."

"So if you felt that way as a football player," I said, "why go into wrestling, where you are totally at the mercy of a promoter? I mean, if he wants, Vince McMahon can squash you."

"Now? I don't think so!" Johnson said, and for the first

time since we sat down he flashed some of The Rock's supreme self-confidence. It took me by surprise. His appetite aside, I was also beginning to notice how . . . I don't know . . . *not* macho Johnson was. From TV, I knew that he was smooth-skinned; now I saw that he shaved or waxed his body hair to achieve this look. Later, looking through pictures in his book, I noticed Johnson even shaved his underarms. And though he was eager to provide careful answers to my questions, we never fell into the swaggering banter usual with athletes. But then athletes, even though they perform in public and must attend to their image, generally do not have superhero alter egos completely supplanting themselves. Wondering what it must be like, I asked Johnson if there were times he wished he were not The Rock.

"Nah," he said. "There's no other Rock out there. I don't think I'll ever get tired of it."

But if many women (like his former WWE colleague Chyna) had gotten tired of always being on display, of being told that their worth depended entirely on their looks, did it not bother him, a man, being objectified in that way? That was not how I put it to him, though. Instead, I read something Sylvester Stallone had said. For two decades, from *Rocky* to *Rambo*, Stallone had been the paragon of muscle-bound manhood, just as Johnson was looking like he would be for the next decade. But by the nineties, the emptiness behind the façade of brawn began to rankle Stallone. He, the man, had been lost to the image. "I just want to play me," he complained, telling Susan Faludi that he was ready to take off the macho mask he had been wearing since the mid-seventies. "You've got it," Stallone said, referring to his famous physique, "but it comes out in this vanity thing which borders on the world of exotic dancing with women. You qualify for nothing—like the Chippendales dancers. . . . It's like the orchid; it's so gorgeous but it's a parasite. It lives off of everything but what it is."

Johnson's handlers had twice come over to our table in an effort to end the interview; each time, Johnson shooed them away. Seeing that I was reading aloud from a big book on the "betrayal of the American man," they made a third appearance. "We're cool," Johnson said. He was not cool with Stallone's self-criticism, however. "I don't feel that way," he said emphatically. "I don't have a lot of conflict about what I do. Not to that extent. Actually, not at all. I try to be as simple as possible. It is what it is. I get it."

He would repeat that last sentence several times. That wrestling was a con, that wrestlers were fetish objects, that despite the macho posturing it was all an exercise in effete vanity, that the goal of the whole farrago was to arouse anxieties that the purchase of a pay-per-view broadcast or a bobblehead doll promised to placate. . . . He got it. Or at least he told me he did. Careful not to say anything that would hurt his image, Johnson let me do most of the talking. He didn't disagree with my theories on professional wrestling and the cult of celebrity, but neither did he admit to any misgivings.

"I'm very proud of the commodity, of the brand I've built," he said. "I understand what it's all about. I get it."


NOT MANY PEOPLE did get it, though—including, it seems, Johnson's employers.

In January 2001, World Wrestling Entertainment inaugurated a professional football league with the help of $100 million from NBC. The XFL it was called. The X stood for "extreme," supposedly. Turns out, the only thing extreme was the hype. Promised blood and guts, an astonishing fifteen million viewers tuned in for the first broadcast. The critics pounced, though. The broadcast was a "bad dream," they said, a "shameful" moment in television history. "It was one of the most mindless things I have ever seen," said the priggish Bob Costas. Actually, it was just an unexciting blowout of a football game. Though fans feigned manic enthusiasm for the camera, the play was real enough, and that was the problem.

Nevertheless, in the run-up to the league's launch, WWE executives spoke confidently of their "highly integrated marketing machine" to create the sort of imagery and slogans that people would pay to have on a T-shirt. "We know what we are doing with the XFL," chief financial officer Augie Liguri told me, extolling the company's "core competencies" in marketing, merchandizing, and licensing. They also had the advantage of working with a built-in, self-identifying, brand-loyal audience. "The critics who are saying we will never be able to do this don't know a thing about our demographic," Vince McMahon said.

By the second week of the season, as ratings began to plummet to the lowest ever for prime-time network television, it seemed clear that for once neither did McMahon. It was true that pro sports had snubbed the "hard-hat, lunch-pail" fan, as McMahon alleged. But, generally speaking, the wrestling fans of his vaunted demographic were not stereotypical blue-collar workers, trudging off to the manufacturing plant. In the past, they might have been, but most now worked in the service industry. And just as wrestlers only played at being athletes, they played at being sports fans, using the butch tropes of athletics to cover for a queeny diva-idolatry. Baseball, basketball, and football clearly had their share of prima donnas. Yet despite all of the pomp, legitimate sports were still basically rooted in reality. And that wasn't good enough for wrestling fans; they wanted to be assured of an over-the-top melodramatic experience.

So did the wrestlers, having little interest in subordinating their vanity to a team or the rigors of competition. Though naturally athletic and endowed with tremendous size and strength, Dwayne Johnson quit his high school wrestling team after a day, concluding that it was boring. "I was more of an entertainer than a wrestler," he admits. Both in his book and in our conversation, Johnson talked a lot about the media attention he had received while playing football for the University of Miami. He didn't say much about his athletic accomplishments, perhaps because there was not much to say. He seemed to consider his publicity the more important accomplishment, and it galled him that his coaches weren't duly impressed. "Even as a second-string player I got more press than anyone!" he said, the bitterness coming back to him. "I gave good interviews! But for some reason, I always got this shitty vibe from the coaches. Now that I think about it, I was head and shoulders above them, and they felt uncomfortable about that."

The difficulties Johnson encountered in college provided an object lesson in what the image culture was all about. He and his coaches weren't playing the same game. To them, what a player did on the field mattered. To Johnson, it didn't, not really. Getting attention did, and that was mostly a function of perception, of putting a performance over.

You didn't have to be an athlete; you just had to play one.

And as President George W. Bush proved, you needn't have been a soldier to seem heroic; you just had to dress up like one.

This Johnson got.

# CHAPTER NINE

DO I HAVE TO ARM WRESTLE YOU TO HAVE A
RELATIONSHIP WITH YOU AS ANOTHER MAN?

—JOHN LENNON

**K**EEP ON BRAGGING, keep on sassing, and always be outrageous," was the advice Gorgeous George gave a braggy young boxer named Cassius Clay in 1961. By then, Gorgeous George had become a favorite of the stripper Gypsy Rose Lee, one of the early camp icons. At a show in Las Vegas in the 1950s, they and Lou Thesz played their burlesque to perfection. Gorgeous George pranced around the ring like a princess. But when Rose planted a long kiss

**OPPOSITE:** JOHN CHAVEZ, AKA ANGEL, THE
HARDCORE HOMO

163

on Thesz, Gorgeous George got jealous—of her. He threw a rose to the ground and was about to slap the man-stealing hussy when Thesz stepped in to protect her. The fight ensued.

Here was the dialectic of wrestling distilled to its essence: attraction expressed as aggression. Gorgeous George was actually a tough and talented technical wrestler, a beer-drinking regular guy, well liked by his colleagues, and not effete or gay. But like Dwayne Johnson a half-century later, he had an intuition of what wrestling was really about—masculinity, male intimacy, and fear. The spectacle has never stopped playing variations on those themes, enacting a drama of homosocial (if not homosexual) affection that demands an equal and opposite insistence on brawn, babes, and, above all, brutality. "It's a very gay sport," a WWE spokesman told the *Village Voice* in 2000, "and to keep it macho, homophobia must be and is incited." A wrestler did not necessarily have to understand, as Johnson and Gorgeous George clearly did, that the macho posturing and gay taunting were an expression of the same anxiety. He just had to embody that anxiety.

And an awful lot of them did. Johnson hadn't answered the question that had been nagging at me—namely, why would boys who were anxious to prove their masculinity embrace the traditionally feminine arts of display and ornamentation?—but his spectacular success suggested one explanation. A culture that offered men few ways to prove themselves besides vanity inevitably fostered narcissistic worries about appearance. For many young wrestlers, I think, there was a certain unconscious embarrassment in this. Most of them overcompensated to a ridiculous degree, turning themselves into living cartoons of masculinity—"living the gimmick," as their more astute fans observed. At the same time, though, they were stuck in a spectacular irony. What they hoped to say about themselves and what they in fact said were diametrically opposed. They wanted to be seen as the embodiment of heterosexual manliness, yet the man-on-man antics betrayed them.

It was, I believe, a matter not of ignorance but of an unresolved inner conflict, both in them and in the culture. The melodramas of hardcore professional wrestling were their way of wrestling with that conflict. Like the shoplifter whose real hope is to get caught in the act, thereby validating a guilt he already feels, young wrestlers couldn't seem to help themselves from being caught out in patently queer situations. Even with the assistance of ghostwriters, their bestselling autobiographies returned again and again to genital concerns. The creative streak that Mick Foley showed in high school, for instance, writing ditties about his or a friend's nether regions (he and four friends called themselves the Brothers Penis), continued through college, with the making of short films that involved much grabbing of testicles. His songs typically ended with someone chopping off the male member; likewise, the movies depicted a lovelorn Foley committing suicide. Unlike the emasculated penis, however, the dead Foley comes back to life transformed, a swaggering stud named Dude Love—"a laid-back cat . . . my fantasy creation of what a man was supposed to be."

Conscious, perhaps, of the fine line between identification and desire, Foley would be less forthcoming about a related fantasy. Telling his college friends that he had a girlfriend in another town, every weekend he'd drive twenty hours and a thousand miles to get intimate (i.e., train) with a man in Freedom, Pennsylvania. After months of getting "slammed, hip-tossed, and suplexed" without mercy, he began to gain confidence, but still was not ready to out himself. "Wrestling was something I wanted to keep just to myself," he says.

That was in 1986, when wrestling was still considered deviant and disreputable. It has since "come out of the closet," writes Dwayne Johnson in *The Rock Says*. Fans are no longer so embarrassed as to keep "their fetish" to themselves, he says.

The fetish Johnson referred to was none other than himself—a man who spoke of serving his opponents "a big double rock burger with extra rock sauce on the side." In case the reader was not clear what form of sodomy Johnson has in mind by this piece of descriptive writing, he clarifies the matter: "Instead of shoving it down Stone Cold Steve Austin's throat, the Rock would have shoved it up his candy ass." Another point of clarification: the wrestling is rough ("The average man needs at least a week to recover from a date with The Rock," he brags) but consensual.

To illustrate, Johnson describes his so-called championship bout with World Wrestling Entertainment's other star of the moment, Stone Cold Steve Austin, at WrestleMania XV. Johnson knew he would "drop the belt" (lose the championship) and didn't mind since he and Austin were close. "I trusted him and he trusted me," he says, and they enjoyed working out the choreography leading up to the "climactic" moment in the ring. On this night, at Philadelphia's First Union Center, after about twenty minutes of the usual rigmarole, Austin kicked out of a finishing move called "The Rock Bottom," then evaded "The People's Elbow," and delivered his own "Stone Cold Stunner" to win the match.

"Did Stone Cold Steve Austin give The Rock all he could

handle?" Johnson asks. "Did The Rock give Stone Cold all *he* could handle . . . and then some? You're damn right he did."

Back in the locker room, in a shift from the third person to the first, the he-man ferocity becomes a moment of post-coital tenderness. "I was drenched with sweat. An odd blend of euphoria and exhaustion enveloped me," Johnson writes.

> The door flew open and in walked Steve Austin. He tossed the belt—*his belt, now*—onto the couch. I jumped to my feet and met him in the center of the room, and we hugged for a good ten seconds. It was a strong hug, a real fucking brotherly embrace reflecting a tacit understanding that we had just shared something remarkable.
>
> "Thank you," Steve said.
>
> "Thank *you*. It was my pleasure."
>
> As we released our hug, we both fell into the couch, completely spent.

NO WONDER young men were beating one another silly. Nowhere else did they gather in such great numbers to watch a show of nearly naked men tussling in one another's arms until, in the end, they lay on the mat like exhausted lovers. It had to be unsettling, if only unconsciously, watching a kind of highly ritualized performance of male intercourse. The wrestlers helped fight off their anxieties, in the ring. They were big and muscular and, therefore, taken as the quintessence of virile masculinity. Very often, too, a wrestler had a buxom babe by his side. But like the referee, her essential role was to be rendered *in*essential, irrelevant, something to be ignored, gotten rid of.

"Get her out of the building, she never belonged in the first place," Jesse Ventura would shout at Macho Man Randy Savage's personal "valet," Miss Elizabeth. "Now we'll get down to wrestling."

About that, Hulk Hogan was in total agreement. "Yes, I've got lust," he would say. "But it's not for Elizabeth. I've got lust for you, Macho Man."

At best, a girl who dreamed of a career in wrestling—rarely as a wrestler but as what they called eye candy—could only hope to play a beard, covering the elaborate courtship rituals between men. Even Zicari had little use for the few female porn stars in the XPW locker room. Women may have

sold pornography, but Zicari knew that when it came to wrestling, fans only had eyes for men.

For years, the most popular wrestler on the indie scene was James Fullington, "the original hardcore icon," who made his entrance to Metallica's hard-driving heavy metal anthem "Enter Sandman"—hence his character's name. Tall, blond, and ruggedly handsome, Sandman looked like a onetime high school quarterback gone to pot, which is exactly what he was: a guy who never outgrew the simple pleasures of his misspent youth. His costume was a studiously simple macho getup of baggy jeans, T-shirt, and construction boots. No makeup, no tights, no long hair. The one esoteric touch was his Singapore whipping cane. "That's basically me," Fullington once told me backstage at a show in Ohio. "Ask anyone and they'll tell you: I'm the straightest shooter in the business; I always say exactly how I fuckin' feel. That's why fans relate to me. This is my life. I fuckin' wake up around noon, smoke pot, ride my Harley, smoke pot, go to the fucking tanning booth, smoke pot, pick the kids up from school, smoke pot. . . . Basically, drinking and smoking pot was the reason I got into wrestling. Ninety percent of the time, I'm fucking smashed before I go into the ring. I once wrestled on a half-gallon of vodka. I got completely naked in the ring, except for my boots. I had my cane between my balls. . . ."

Such were Fullington's airs and affects. Like Steve Austin, he played at being a working stiff, but really his shtick was to deliberately disregard the work ethic. Even among his colleagues he was not considered "a worker"—a wrestler who could physically work a match with a repertoire of choreographed and rehearsed holds. He merely played the role of one, wearing the costume, lugging a ten-foot aluminum ladder around the arena, stopping here and there to climb to the top, open a can of beer, and take a hearty swig, as his theme song blared:

*Take my hand,*
*we're off to never never land . . .*

The teenage boys in the audience gathered ecstatically at his feet, the telephoto lenses of their point-and-shoot cameras coming to life like little penises. The teenage boys watching with their mouths agape, Fullington vigorously shook a can of beer down by his crotch before popping the tab. This was typically the supreme moment of the entire evening: the boys fighting to get a mouthful of Sandman's elixir, which, from certain angles, looked like a rain of urine.

"I got a beer bath!" a scrawny kid once said, high-fiving me in giddy glee. "I'm a bitch for Sandman!"

Few if any fans saw the sexual symbolism of the performance. They just thought that Sandman was cool, and longed to emulate his rebellious swagger. And anyway, they averred, nothing so fiercely violent could possibly be queer. Wrestling was a sport, "a contact sport," Urial Yakobov insisted. "We're just hoping to see a little action, that's all. It's not gay. Trust me. It's wrestling."

But why *this* action? Why even go there? If they were looking for aggressive athletic competition, it wasn't like they had no other options. What did professional wrestling offer that boxing, hockey, football, or amateur wresting didn't?

Vengeance, for one thing.

"Let's say you're tag-teaming and your partner turns you

on—I mean, he turns on you. You're gonna want revenge," is how one fan explained the matter to me.

"Your average fan wants to express all those homophobic feelings because . . . well, just think about it," the wrestler John Chavez explained. "Here you have two guys in their underwear holding each other in locks, all sweaty and everything. Even the real manly man looks kind of gay grabbing some guy's crotch. And the fan, instead of being out with a girl on a Saturday night, is there with a whole bunch of guys, watching other guys. And when he thinks about that, like, unconsciously, it makes him feel a little weird. He wants to be like the big rugged guy. So he's thinking, 'If I beat up a gay guy—that proves I'm not gay.' Since he's not supposed to do that, it's just as satisfying watching someone else do it."

Chavez went by the name Angel, which took advantage of his Mexican heritage but also of a certain softness and delicacy in his demeanor. Though not actually gay, Chavez worked the clichés of fey boy-toy homosexuality for all they were worth, becoming known as "The Hardcore Homo."

Why, then, did fans cheer and not jeer him?

"I don't know," said Chavez. "They're supposed to hate me, but they don't. I'm getting a shine."

"A shine?"

"A pop, a rise out of the crowd."

"So to speak."

"And," he said, "I'm always getting hit on after shows."

"As a joke?"

"For real!"

ALL IT TOUGH LOVE—a love that suddenly, surprisingly, was daring to speak its name. For decades after Paul Boesch introduced the idea in Houston, in the late 1930s, tag teams were just an occasional novelty act. But with the story lines that began developing in the mid-1990s, in which wrestlers were seen teaming up to supposedly overtake a promotion or settle old "behind-the-scenes" scores, tag teams had been growing in appeal. It was always a curious phenomenon, though. A tag team in the eighties made a perverse show of licking each other's faces. Others hugged and fondled each other. Even the butch partnerships like Steve Austin and Brian Pillman's "Hollywood Blondes" were marriages of true minds refusing to admit impediments. Historically, there was nothing remarkable in any of this. In ancient Rome and Alexandria, homosexual lovers were considered the ideal warriors, since it was believed they were motivated by the noblest of sentiments—the love and admiration of another man. Usually, though, the love of males at the sentimental heart of wrestling escaped awareness. When Hunter Hearst Helmsley told his "buddy" Shawn Michaels, "You are weak, you are vulnerable; that's why I wanted you by my side—so I could have protected you," nobody seemed to think anything of it. Was that because the violence masked the affection? Because Shawn Michaels was supposedly so successful with the ladies? Or because he was able to tell Triple H, "I'm going to show my little boy that sometimes you got to fight to be a man"?

I didn't know who, or what, Michaels meant by his "little boy." All I knew was that wrestling was "where the big boys play," as WCW used to say—boys who gave themselves names like Val Venis, Prince Albert (slang for penis piercing), Macho

Man (an homage, one presumes, to the Village People), Big Sexy (sexy to whom if not the mostly male audience?), and Mr. Ass (famous for pointing to his bulging bikini, as his fans yelled, "Suck it!"). And, of course, there was the biggest boy of them all, Hulk Hogan, resembling nothing so much as an engorged phallus. "I want to know if you can handle the largest arms in the world around your waist?" he would ask his opponents.

In September 2002, a week after the *New York Times* began publishing same-sex wedding announcements, the WWE's writers, hip to the obvious subtext of wrestling, decided to make homosexual love the text itself with the tag team Chuck and Billy, the first conspicuously queer characters who were not seen as cruisin' for a bruisin'. Getting down on one knee, Chuck proposed to a tearful Billy (née Mr. Ass). As it happens, the couple never actually exchanged vows (at the last minute, they revealed that they were straight and, naturally, proceeded to beat the crap out of each other), but the good-humored routine earned praise from the Gay & Lesbian Alliance Against Defamation. Even more remarkable, it met with fan approval. A sense of camp had made the subject safe.

"It's not gay," wrestlers would say, "it's kicking ass." But, of course, they were not really kicking ass; they were collaborating. "It's very much like dancing, like doing a waltz," says Jesse Ventura. Marlon "Tiger" Kahn, who worked for the short-lived revival of Stampede Wrestling in Calgary, described the matches in the lowly minor leagues, where nobody made much money, as a kind of exercise in foreplay. "We tickle each other, we bite each other, we pull each other's pants down—whatever it takes to enjoy ourselves, usually ending in one big cluster fuck," he said. Others have also likened their matches to "making love." Dick "The Destroyer" Breyer, a masked wrestler from the fifties and sixties, says: "Trying to get the crowd enthused and excited—it's kind of like being in bed with a young lady. You want to get that girl excited but not that excited right off the bat. So you stick it in just a little and she starts to get excited, see. And then you pull it out, see. Then you stick it back in, and you go back a little bit harder, see. Finally, you really get it going, and when she comes— that's the finish of the wrestling match."

Even if it was a woman they were "making love" to, the analogy was telling—not that wrestlers and their fans were all closeted homosexuals (nobody within the business seemed to regard the few who are openly gay with alarm), but that wrestling was shot through with sexual anxiety.

That anxiety, as any criminal psychologist will attest, is the cause of much of the violence they see in prisons. There, men sexually assault other men to prove, paradoxically, their own manliness. In professional wrestling, men don't really rape one another. They just pretend to, for laughs. But why? What could be the point? Why create homoerotic skits night after night?

The point, I think, was the same as in prison assaults—to temporarily restore self-esteem, the fans' and the wrestlers' own, by transforming latent shame into manifest pride through the medium of violence. Though few young men could see that the vamping for attention was perhaps unbecoming to them as men, most of them felt the frustration and humiliation of failing to measure up to an image culture's ideas of success. As much as they wanted to be part of that culture, they also wanted to exact revenge. Participating in the sadomasochistic rituals of pro wrestling, even as fans, was one way of doing both.

THE HARDCORE HOMO

But there was a heaping dollop of humor and irony to those rituals, and it helped wrestlers deal with the incongruities between fantasy and reality. Like the stereotypical drag queen whose dressing up as a woman provided both an escape *from* and recognition *of* the fundamental fact of the matter (that, in the end, he was still a man), the wrestler's manly shtick was an admission of defeat—an empowering and liberating admission, however, in which aggression took the form of play, play that masked but also reconciled deeper concerns and conflicts.

"In naïve, or pure, Camp the essential element is seriousness, a seriousness that fails," Susan Sontag says. Later in her famous essay on the subject, she says something slightly different: "Camp is playful, anti-serious. More precisely, Camp involves a new, more complex relation to 'the serious.'" To Christopher Isherwood, camp is a way of "expressing what's basically serious to you in terms of fun and artifice and elegance."

Something along these paradoxical lines was going on with the "exquisite mayhem" of professional wrestling. What it means to be tough, to be a man—for a teenage boy, this was very serious stuff. How is he to seek attention without seeming fey? How can he square the seeming inconsistency of a cult of manliness with an effeminate attention to image and ornamentation? These are not easy matters for a boy to figure out. Nor are they trivial. His entire sense of himself is wrapped up in them. He is looking for answers, and professional wrestling may not provide them as such. But amid all of the buffoonery and grotesqueries, wrestling's rites and rituals at least present him with a reading of his anxieties.

What he learns is what his culture's ethos and his private sensibility (or, anyway, certain aspects of them) look like when spelled out externally in a collective text; that the two are near enough alike to be articulated in the symbolics of a single such text; and—the disquieting part—that the text in which this revelation is accomplished consists of a man beating another to a bloody pulp.

I have again quoted anthropologist Clifford Geertz on the subject of the Balinese cockfight, changing his last phrase ("a chicken hacking another mindlessly to bits") to suit professional wrestling. In Bali, it is chickens, not grown men, that function as the fetish objects through which men mediate their deepest concerns. There, villagers speak to one another through their cocks. Here, young men speak to one another through flamboyantly theatrical men like The Rock.

This is an understandably sensitive subject for a seventeen-year-old boy. By the time he figures out that there is something awfully swish about the concept of tag teams, say, he is probably finished with wrestling. It has served its purpose. He has dealt with his "homo angst," as Rob Zicari called this time in a boy's life. Meantime, the boy yelling "Kill the faggot!" and "You like men!" is very likely the same boy carrying a scrapbook bulging with magazine cutouts and eight-by-ten glossies of his favorite male wrestlers, crying, "We want head!" He doesn't recognize his obsessions as crushes because he doesn't think of himself as gay. In fact, he probably isn't gay. But he is intensely interested in manliness, in what it means and how to emulate it. Worried about not having the stuff that men are made of, he turns to totemic figures for possible solutions to his anxieties. And as much as this fetish betrays his fears, it also seems to guard against them.

# CHAPTER TEN

WE ARE CRUDE AND SORROWFUL AND SUPERFI-
CIAL—I BELIEVE WE ARE LOST.

—ERICH MARIA REMARQUE

**B**OYS ARE CONSTANTLY being told that nothing is ever solved by violence. They know better, though. They know that a great deal is solved, at least temporarily. An act of violence saves face. It defeats humiliation. It diminishes psychic pain. It gives one a sense of pride and power. It commands attention. It covers for insecurities. A genuine contest of athletic supremacy would only get in the way of the ultimate purpose of that violence. As in the flogging and scarification rites of the Mehinaku Indians in Brazil,

OPPOSITE: WIFEBEATER

say, or of Sambia boys in New Guinea, the important thing is to prove that you can take a beating. Thus, actual injuries to the flesh are enormously important as symbols. The wounds signal inner anguish and serve to authenticate honor and dignity and manliness. Above all, a wound is a prerequisite to healing.

This is the paradoxical logic to every wrestling match. Wrestlers are trying to win for themselves, and for their audience, a feeling of importance achieved through violence. To prompt that violence, they invite feelings of weakness and victimization. To be healed, they first have to suffer.

It is a peculiar phenomenon but hardly unique to pro wrestling. In the 1990s, America became a nation of victims, and every one of them seemed compelled to write about it. Witness the popularity of Dave Pelzer's three memoirs of his horrific abuse as a child, which has stayed on the *New York Times* nonfiction paperback bestseller list for a combined total of ten years. In *A Child Called It*, the first of his books, Pelzer describes in vivid Technicolor detail his mother smearing shit in his face, making him eat his own vomit, stabbing him, starving him, and forcing him to drink ammonia. Total fantasy, family members say, but the story obviously had enormous appeal to the daytime television crowd. "You just want to make them happy," Pelzer says, and apparently by telling fantastic stories of victimization he has.

The wrestler Mick Foley's stab at fiction, *Tietam Brown*, failed to strike a similar chord with a mass audience—a surprise, no doubt, to his publishers, considering that Foley's first two memoirs topped the *Times*'s bestseller list. Although spectacularly imbecilic, the novel makes for interesting reading as a kind of specimen dream. The boy who narrates the story is molested and maimed for life. He witnesses the killing of two foster mothers (one is decapitated in a car crash, the other blows her brains out). When two boys in an orphanage force him to perform oral sex, he bites off the testicles of one and kills the other with a punch to the Adam's apple. At seventeen, he is taken in by the racist father he has never known, a former professional wrestler who rapes his neighbors and celebrates Christmas with a vengeance. In school, a steroidal history teacher calls him a fag and delivers a crushing blow to his face. Nevertheless, in calling Abraham Lincoln a "cocksucker," the boy wins the angelic heart of a chesty preacher's daughter who calls him "Big Boy." Soon another boy—a boy who, incidentally, is busy raping his own mom on the side—sexually assaults the girl. Meanwhile, it turns out that our hero's father had murdered the boy's mother, and soon commences ripping his son's shoulder and thumb from their sockets. Finally, the kid ends up in a mental hospital, captive to a sodomizing psychiatrist.

The story is just a fantasy, but what a revealing fantasy it is! That Foley imagined getting raped and maimed is hardly surprising for a professional wrestler; every show, night after night, year after year, returns to the same scenario of humiliation and victimization. Naturally, the masochistic wish these degradation ceremonies fulfill is well disguised in a lot of macho clowning; the drama also satisfies the opposite sadistic fantasy, for vengeance. Really, though, the two scenarios are a bifurcation of a single unconscious wish, one in which aggression is inextricable from affection. And the fact that the simplistic story of a good guy fighting a bad guy has to be endlessly played out suggests that fans (and perhaps many of the wrestlers) are still trying to sort out these incoherent and contradictory emotions. Just as a small child will ask to hear the same bedtime story again and again until he has worked through the emotional issues it touches on, wrestling fans never seem to mind or even notice the repetitiveness of the matches so long as they correlate with their inner conflicts.

Needless to say, wrestling isn't *Sesame Street*—a production dreamt up by educators and child psychologists to teach boys how to deal with the problems of becoming men in a complex world. But staging shows nonstop over the course of more than a century now, promoters have learned what speaks to audiences and what only confuses them. Wrestling has endured because it responds to what young men are dealing with, consciously and unconsciously.

S O AFTER fifteen years of taking some of the nastiest bumps in the history of the business, Mick Foley was able to say in writing what he and every other wrestler had tried to say—and gainsay—in the ring: that despite how tough he was, he really just wanted to be weak and vulnerable, to be loved and taken care of, like a child. Few of Foley's admirers, however, have his facility with words (such as it is). Even if they did, without his fame, they are unlikely to get book deals with prestigious publishers.

What they had instead was pro wrestling. For lack of anything better, this is their medium of communication.

"The whole attitude is about saying, 'Fuck you—I don't have to follow your rules,'" explained the hardcore wrestler Matt Prince. "It's kind of ridiculous, but it's also kind of liberating, like having Tourette's syndrome. You have license to say whatever you want."

Matt Prince worked for the Philadelphia-based Combat Zone Wrestling, going by the name Wifebeater, which pretty well described what he looked like—a brute who slapped his wife around. "She had it coming . . ." went the saying on the T-shirts he sold at shows. In fact, though, Prince was never less than a prince of a guy, quiet and courteous with his fellow wrestlers, his girlfriend, and me. At the same time, he had been a brawler ever since he could remember. "Sometimes after going out and getting fucked up and in fights, I'll have to walk home at, like, five in the morning, and I'll get thinking about why I do it," he told me before one of his epic death matches in the Mecca of hardcore wrestling, Philly's Viking Hall. "Mainly I just like the sheer weirdness of it. I don't take it seriously."

Maybe not, but he was serious about proving something to himself, he just was not quite sure what. A year after graduating from high school—a year of drinking, taking drugs, committing petty crimes, and not knowing what else to do with his life—Prince enlisted in the Marines, thinking it would test his mettle as a man. But basic training at Camp Lejeune, in North Carolina, was not the manly ordeal that popular myth had made it out to be. "It was definitely disappointing," he said. "They talk like the Marines are this elite fighting force, but unless you're a total pussy you're going to get through it. It's just not that tough."

The tough part would come after basic training. With no wars to fight at that time—this was before 9/11—being a Marine, for Prince, seemed mostly a matter of doing his time, ironing his uniform, making beds, and picking up litter. They were the few, the proud, the tidy. Depressed, he would hit nearby Jacksonville's massage parlors, getting serviced by Asian women ("their hands are smaller, which makes your dick look bigger," he explained), or drive home to Philadelphia on weekends, staying up drinking the entire time, waiting till the very last minute to report for duty. Returning late after one of those debauched weekends, Prince started behaving strangely crazy. "I started brushing my teeth all the time, and just told them some weird crap. I told them that breathing wasn't automatic for me, that I couldn't stop thinking of my grandmother naked. Shit like that. And they locked me up in a hospital and gave me some cool drugs. Valium and stuff. I just lay around in my pajamas for a couple of months, and then they gave me an honorable medical discharge with a big disability payment—close to ten grand. I spent it all on pussy and beer."

I believe it is this sort of longing—grandmothers, pajamas, bed, easeful narcosis—that psychiatrists mean by the term "infantile regression." Problem was, it seldom lasts. Pussy and beer Prince could always get. He still had to figure out how to satisfy what he considered perfectly natural and normal aggressive impulses and, in the process, certify himself as a man. Beating the crap out of another guy—it was not the sort of thing a civilized society encouraged, even if the fighting was mutual, mostly in fun, and served an ulterior purpose. Playing pro sports was not an option. Tough as he was, Prince had never been much of an athlete, and it riled him that he had been duped into believing that sports would be his express ticket to wealth and fame. "You grow up thinking you're going to be this great athlete, but I wasn't even that good on my Little League team," he said. "So unless you're Michael Jordan, it's all about posturing." And though he couldn't begin to say how much he absolutely hated the idea of posing, part of him recognized that his fighting was just that—a way of "acting" real manly. "It's like we're all trying to be the peacock with the brightest feathers that gets to bang all the chicks and that all of the other peacocks think is cool," he said. "I get all the benefits of being a pretty boy without having to *be* a pretty boy."

Everything about Prince, from the torn jeans to the work boots to the welter of scars on his back and chest, seemed opposed to glamour and display. Although he has spent a lot of time in the gym, taking particular pride in the massive slabs of his shoulder and back muscles, he disparaged the prissy preoccupation so many men have with their bodies. "Maybe self-improvement isn't the answer," writes Chuck Palahniuk; and Prince was a wrestler after that novelist's heart. In *Fight Club*, Palahniuk created a kind of born-again movement of young men rediscovering their manhood by rejecting the body-beautiful ethos, ritually beating the shit out of one another instead. A fan of the movie adaptation, Prince was a more plausible version of the character played by the miscast Brad Pitt (a pretty boy if ever there was one). He looked like someone who genuinely believed that ridiculous acts of self-destruction were the answer to what he called the "wussification of America."

What Prince got from *Fight Club* was not the idea of getting into senseless fights—that much he had figured out for himself—but a philosophy that recast his anger and aggression into righteous indignation. "We are the middle children of history, raised by television to believe that someday we'll be millionaires and movie stars and rock stars, but we won't," Palahniuk writes. "We're just learning this fact. So don't fuck with us."

"Exactly!" Prince said when I called him up one night and quoted the passage. "We're all fucking pissed off. And this"—hardcore professional wrestling, he meant—"is our way of saying 'Fuck you!' We have nothing. This is the best thing we've figured out. We're a bunch of miserable, angry fucking bastards—guys who are uglier than most guys, who are unathletic, who never got the girl, society's outcasts, saying, 'I just don't give a fuck.' I don't care about my body, and I definitely don't care about *your* body."

YOU'LL NEVER see the repertoire of traditional holds and reversals in a Wifebeater match. Wifebeater doesn't even bother with the pretenses of competition. The ropes are usually taken down and barbed wire is strung in their place. Beds of barbed wire, along with beds of fluorescent light tubes, are also placed in the corners and on the cement floor. Strewn about the ring are "weapons" that fans bring from home, made out of old TVs, stereos, and various household appliances, typically involving yet more glass, more thumbtacks, and more barbed wire. Then, without any further ado—and without ever speaking to or acknowledging the crowd—Wifebeater enters the arena like a bull, head down, shoulders hunched, brow furrowed, and, stepping into the ring, immediately begins bashing his opponent, and getting pulverized in return, with whatever implement happens to be handy.

My description sounds rather perfunctory, and in a way the action is unthinkingly mechanical—the wrestlers are simply following the standard choreography—but in a matter of minutes, blood will have covered Wifebeater's entire face, back, arms, and chest. The cement floor around the ring becomes viscous and slippery with pools of blood—blood that will have splattered all over my shirt, my glasses, my camera lens, blood that boys in the crowd anoint themselves with as the fight spills out of the ring and over the metal barricades.

Only after Wifebeater has jumped from every possible perch in Viking Hall, after breaking through countless particleboard tables, after all of the "weapons" have been deployed and destroyed, after a weed whacker has been unleashed against Wifebeater's back and chest, after he and his opponent have become hopelessly entangled in barbed wire—only then does an official inspector from the state athletic commission, acting as a kind of deus ex machina, step in and end the match, usually with a disqualification.

P AIN CAN BE a cause of delight," the British polemicist Edmund Burke wrote in 1759. And bodily pain, in particular, "is productive of the sublime."

So what sublime message, I asked Prince, did shredding his flesh raw by a weed whacker communicate?

"I don't know—maybe that, if it removes your nipple, like it did mine, the nipple will grow back," he said.

"Excuse me?"

"Yeah," he said, "it kind of surprised me, too."

"Well, it wasn't like you really needed it," I said.

"No, but it looks more symmetrical this way."

So, yes. There was that.

More importantly, I think the weed whacker gave Prince an identity: he was the star of his own Passion Play.

Self-mutilation is usually thought to be a sign of mental anguish, a muted form of suicide. But men have always inflicted injuries to their bodies for socially sound reasons. Deliberate and ritual body modification is not just common in tribal communities, it is often fundamental. The young are made to pass through episodes of pain and suffering on the way to adulthood. The devoutly religious also mortify their flesh. And while the millions of marathon runners are not drawing blood, they, too, are engaging in a form of self-injury. In all these cases, agony is thought to be an agent of self-help and self-improvement, the price one must pay for greater emotional and spiritual rewards. "Pain is weakness leaving the body," they say in the Marines. For the sick of heart, pain is also self-expression, a way of symbolizing feelings that often can't be put in words.

Prince himself eventually came to understand that his masochistic performances were more a matter of revealing weakness than strength. "I think, 'I'll fuck myself up, maybe that'll get the sympathy I really want,' " he said. "That's one of the reasons it's hard to be a man today. To be masculine, you almost have to fake it."

Matt Prince was no fool. He also figured out pretty quickly that even if his performance was an attack on celebrity, he, in his own small way, was participating in that culture, creating his own daft fame. "You can't buy the experience," he admitted. "Before wrestling, I had never signed an autograph. Nobody I know had ever signed an autograph. All of a sudden, you're interesting, you're cool, you're doing something that sets you apart from the average person. To want that is natural. I mean, everybody wants to be the star of his own life. The guy who works at McDonald's thinks he's the most important person in the world, too."

So he hadn't been completely honest with himself when we first spoke. Like most young men his age, he did give a fuck—enough, anyway, to savage his body for a little attention. True, his celebrity was limited to a few thousand fans of hardcore wrestling, but it was fame all the same, and for a while it felt fantastic. It proved to him what he had never been sure of—that while he may not be the best looking guy in the world, or the most athletic, or the smartest, he still possessed something special: the drama of his own pain and suffering. And if participating in barbaric sacrificial rites for a few hundred bucks in front of a few hundred shockhead fans in a ratty warehouse directly beneath the busiest interstate on the Eastern seaboard gave him this sense of self-worth, just imagine how extraordinary he would feel performing the same stunts for millions of dollars, in front of millions of people watching on television, dating supermodels, living an incredible life— one of society's privileged sons.

# CHAPTER ELEVEN

> WHOEVER FIGHTS MONSTERS SHOULD SEE TO IT
> THAT IN THE PROCESS HE DOESN'T BECOME A
> MONSTER. —FRIEDRICH NIETZSCHE

O F THE SCORES of wrestling casualties, the one that most fascinated fans was Kerry Von Erich's death, at age thirty-three. He was the son of the legendary Jack Adkisson, who in the fifties and sixties played a goose-stepping Nazi heel going by the Teutonic-sounding name Fritz Von Erich. Running his own promotion out of a dilapidated Dallas arena, Von Erich the elder claimed to have heard a divine voice commanding him to present his sons to the world

OPPOSITE: STU HART AND SMITH HART

191

as paragons of God-fearing, all-American manhood. Soon he had local evangelists announcing female mud-wrestling matches. And with his frequent appearances on Pat Robertson's *700 Club*, he became the first regional promoter since the fifties to reach a national audience, through the Christian Broadcasting Network. Texans (being Texans) went along with the bluster. Von Erich was "godly," journalists wrote. His sons were "home-grown heroes" and "world-renowned" role models. "Tall, trim, powerful young men, they were fundamentally religious, thoroughly sportsmanlike and utterly American" . . . "an unstoppable juggernaut of youth, strength and talent"—especially Kerry, the born-again pinup with the "body of Hercules and the charisma of a rock star."

Despite the death of four of his five brothers (Jackie electrocuted as a child in a freak accident, David and Mike of drug overdoses, Chris of a 9mm bullet to the head), despite losing his right foot in a motorcycle accident (he had been speeding, wearing nothing but gym shorts, when he crashed into the back of a patrol car), despite all the times opponents had carried him through matches in a narcotic stupor, despite the drug arrests, and despite the diminishing crowds, Kerry Von Erich believed in the majesty that a rhinestone-studded championship belt supposedly conferred. He tried to hide the shame of his amputated foot by never removing his right boot, not even in the shower. One day, though, wrestling Colonel DeBeers at a show in Las Vegas, Von Erich was exposed. DeBeers made the mistake of grabbing Von Erich's boot. "The boot came off," writes wrestling historian Dave Meltzer, "revealing a sock without a foot in it."

I think one reason fans and wrestlers have dwelled on Von

Erich's troubles was that, here, they had an objective correlative for his injured psyche: that missing right foot.

"Wrestlers have nothing," says an attorney I know who has given up the practice of law to bootleg wrestling videos. "Once they get into it, they get caught up in the big lie. They become the characters they play. But take away the image and it's like Kerry Von Erich's boot—there's nothing there. Every one of them is full of shit. That's the reason I really dig it."

I agreed. The spectacle of self-delusion made for perverse entertainment, depicting human behavior in its grandiose and grotesque extremes. Celebrity was a high-wire act, and for fans of popular culture, the most interesting part was watching the famous fall—as, inevitably, a few of them do.

T WAS the death of Owen Hart, in May 1999, that brought home just how far professional wrestling had descended into dementia. The business was at the height of its popularity when Hart, dangling some eighty feet above the ring in Kansas City's Kemper Arena, was preparing to introduce himself to the multitudes. "Tonight, darkness will seize the land and destroy all you hold dear," the ghoulish, smoke-shrouded Undertaker proclaimed earlier in the show. Owen Hart was to appear as a preposterously outdated answer to these macabre fascinations. "The Blue Blazer is back because WWE needs The Blue Blazer," Hart told the audience in a pre-taped clip. "The Blue Blazer will triumph over evildoers."

When the Jumbotron clip ended, Hart was supposed to drop from the ceiling, take one step, trip, and fall on his face.

A banana-peel gag. But as he was harnessing himself to the tackle and pulleys from which he would make his spectacular descent, something went horribly wrong. Something slipped, or broke, or failed to catch. What exactly happened was hard to say; it was all over so quickly. Fans saw what looked like a mannequin plummet from the rafters, strike the corner turnbuckle, and flop on its back, eyes wide open.

"This is not part of the entertainment tonight—this is as real as real can be here," ringside announcer Jim Ross told the audience. But what was that supposed to mean in a show whose only reason for being was to blur fact and fantasy? Thrown into a state of giddy confusion, the 16,000 people in the arena continued to chant "Owen! Owen!" waving Styrofoam middle fingers for the cameras as Hart lay staring up into the rafters, his heart no longer beating. They had, after all, come to see men get hurt, and the presence of extras in EMT uniforms tending to wrestlers acting gravely injured was a staple of WWE broadcasts. In fact, the ambulance that Hart would be driven away in had just been used in a skit involving Vince McMahon. And no sooner was Hart out the door than the high jinks resumed, with a wrestler trapping his opponent in a coffin and then smashing the thing with a sledgehammer.

Perhaps to make up for the horrendous judgment of going on with the show even after word came that Hart had died, Vince McMahon decided to broadcast the funeral, against Hart's wife's explicit wishes. In his defense, McMahon pointed out that his company had paid for the video screen, loudspeakers, clothing, and hairdressing necessary for the broadcast. He had also covered the travel expenses of his wrestlers, who, to indicate their sorrow, bashed beer cans together.

It was professional wrestling's truest moment: suffering as spectacle.

"I just found his death very moving," said a fan, explaining why he attended the funeral. "I wouldn't have missed it for anything," said another. "I haven't slept in twenty-four hours, but it's worth it," added a third.

JUST AS the Von Erichs had been in Texas, the Harts were legendary in Canada. When my letters and phone calls to Hart's parents and his brothers and sisters went unanswered, a Calgary telephone operator told me to just show up anyway; anyone in town could tell me where they lived. "They're pretty big around here—in more ways than one, eh?" she said.

So that's what I did.

The operator was right. The first person I asked, a coffee shop barista in downtown Calgary, give me easy directions to the Hart family's Victorian pile seven miles west of downtown. When nobody answered the front door, I followed the sound of grunts and groans coming from an open basement door. Inside, one of Owen's seven older brothers, Bruce, was conducting a training session in a dimly lit twelve-by-twelve-foot room, known as the dungeon. It was here that Stu Hart had trained all eight of his sons and all four of his sons-in-law in the brutalities of wrestling. There was no elevated ring, just some filthy mats on a plywood floor. Instead of bouncing off ropes, the wrestlers crashed into the pine-paneled walls and kicked holes in the low ceiling. The improvised training equipment, jumbled with rusted butcher's knives and saws, seemed designed for medieval forms of torture. Come to think of it, that *was* its purpose; and an experience in pain and suffering was precisely the appeal of training with the brothers Hart.

Six students sitting on old weight-lifting benches had been watching a skinny fifteen-year-old kid getting thrown around by a monstrous French Canadian who called himself Frankenstein (presumably, because that's what he looked like). The action had come to a halt. Dripping sweat, Frankenstein was down on his hands and knees, his face inches from the sweat-soaked, bloodstained, bacteria-infested mat, looking for something. The guys sitting on the weight benches, waiting their turn, told a story about a famous wrestler crapping his pants in the ring. In broken English, a circus strongman from Turkey named Attila asked Bruce if he could say "faggot" in a match.

"Don't worry about that yet," Bruce said.

"Can I say, 'You want my body, bitch?' " Attila asked.

"Not yet," Bruce said.

"Can I say 'motherfucker'?"

"Yes, you can say 'motherfucker.' But right now we're trying to teach you fundamentals."

"I got it!" said Frankenstein, finding a contact lens on the mat. He quickly popped it in his mouth, then his eye, blinking it into place. "Ready!"

"Ready for some more bumps?" Bruce asked.

The kid nodded but looked terrified.

"Drop kick," Bruce began, calling out the shots and bumps as the skinny kid and Frankenstein careened off the walls. "Now a side drop . . . good! A clothesline . . . a nut shot. . . . Don't look so compassionate there! Let's see some facials! Facials are important. . . . Good noise . . . let's keep it rolling. . . . When you're in the middle of a big comeback, guys, it's like sex—you don't want to go limp in the homestretch. . . . Work it! Work the crowd! . . . Okay, finish him off. . . ."

Here were two people pretending to hurt each other, and having a splendid time of it ("it's like sex"). So when another hulk rushed in the room, yanking a woman by her blond hair, I honestly did not think anything of it. Even as everyone else quickly left the room, I stayed, drinking my coffee. I thought that the man and woman were rehearsing one of those backstage domestic-dispute skits you saw every week on WWE's *Raw*. The man was obviously a wrestler—that much I could tell by the fanny pack loosely slung like a codpiece over loose-fitting Zubaz pajama pants, a style many wrestlers had adopted. His skin was also the peculiar shade of purple indicative of steroid abuse. To say that the guy looked like he might explode is, I realize, a cliché. Yet it did seem that his body bulged with more muscles than his skin could possibly contain. One little pinprick, I thought, and he'd burst.

"You're a fucking whore!" he was yelling.

"And you're a fucking drug addict, Davey!"

Davey—that would be the wrestler Davey Boy Smith, a.k.a. The British Bulldog, which meant that this was no skit. The shy, sweet, somewhat dim-witted eighteen-year-old boy with the thick Manchester brogue who had arrived in Calgary twenty years earlier to learn the secrets of strength and valor— that Davey Boy Smith, I knew from other wrestlers, had long ago been written off as yet another drug casualty. Now, like some sort of medieval ogre, he bellowed about how he was going to "do" someone. And for a second there, I thought he was talking about me. But I could have stayed, I could have left, I could have taken pictures, I could have done jumping jacks. Like the dumbbells on the floor, I was just background.

"You gave my dad your word you wouldn't do this anymore," said the woman, whom I now took to be Smith's estranged wife, Diana, the youngest of the Hart daughters.

As if on cue, her ancient father, late into his eighties, entered the dungeon. Amid their screaming and hair-pulling, Stu Hart tried to remind his daughter and son-in-law of the two "bee-uuutiful children" they should be thinking about. But they paid him no attention, either. They kept calling each other whores and drug addicts, kicking and hitting each other, until Davey Boy yanked Diana out the door, body slamming her down on the muddy lawn.

Stu Hart closed the door on them. He had seen it all before, I gathered. "I don't understand this, and I'm too tired for it," he said, and slowly, painfully, walked back upstairs.

HAD WANTED to visit the Harts because, supposedly, they represented the true and valiant heart of professional wrestling. Vince McMahon had re-created wrestling in his own heartless image, critics complained. Whatever was vile and violent and venal about the United States found full expression in WWE, they said. But up in Canada, I had been led to believe, the Hart family still stood for wholesome values. The Hart boys were exemplars of manly honor, supposedly. And in a profession full of scumbags and scalawags, Stu Hart was widely thought to embody the noble virtues of the good guy, the anti-Vince. As a child, he had suffered through subzero winters in a leaky pup tent while his father failed to make a go of it as a farmer on the high plains of western Saskatchewan. Eventually, he would be placed in an Edmonton orphanage. It was there that he discovered submission wrestling. Winning city and provincial championships, he had hoped to compete in the Olympics, until World War II nixed the games. While Hart was on shore leave in Washington, D.C., during his stint in the Royal Canadian Navy, a bald bulldog of a man came up to him on the street, took him by both shoulders, sized him up, and offered him a job. The man was the legendary promoter Toots Mondt. As soon as his navy stint ended, Hart jumped at his offer and was soon earning ninety dollars a week as a wholesome babyface, working in and around New York. "STU HART GETS GALS IN A FLUSTER" read a newspaper headline. "He possesses a boyish charm that will set the feminine hearts a-flutter. . . . Hmmm!"

That charm wasn't lost on Helen Smith, of Long Beach, Long Island. Petite, pretty, and witty, she had been the valedictorian of her high school. Over her mother's objections, on a snowy New Year's Eve, she and Stu married a few months after they met. They would have twelve children in seventeen years.

Stu was not a big reader of classy literature like his wife. He preferred true-life success stories and subscribed to the tenets of a tattered copy of Norman Vincent Peale's *The Power of Positive Thinking*. Later, when he became a promoter, Hart the orphan bought an 8,000-square-foot former orphanage west of downtown Calgary, decorating it with massive chandeliers, Persian carpets, and poofy leather sofas. It was the sort of gaudy grandeur that a poor boy would equate with success. To his wife, the house had always seemed like a seedy hotel.

And with the assortment of odd characters passing through—from Andre the Giant to a wrestling bear that had hibernated under the back porch—not to mention twelve kids and their many cats and dogs, it had become a lot seedier over the years. Broken-down Cadillacs littered the yard, along with washers and driers and dismantled wrestling rings. Without irony, however, the family referred to their home as "the mansion." The Hart children also likened their father as to a god. He prepared the kids' lunches. He did most of the cleaning. He learned to sew. He did his wife's hair. Every Sunday he supervised the shopping and cooking of dinner for seldom less than two dozen people. Kissing his daughters goodnight, he would always growl in their ears like a bear. "My dad ruined us for other men," his daughter Allison said. "I had stars in my eyes."

His eight sons often had stars in their eyes, too, but for a different reason. "I could take all my sons and squash them like maggots," Hart was still saying in his eighties.

From a distance, the Freudian conflicts within the family were as pronounced as the Calgary skyline on the Alberta plains. There was one thing every one of the Harts could agree on, however. The one son whom their father had reason to be proudest of, the son who represented what was best about wrestling itself—its simple, down-to-earth cheerfulness—was Owen.

A S FAR as Bret Hart was concerned, Vince McMahon had all but murdered his little brother, Owen. In his heyday, Bret was considered Canada's third-most-famous "athlete" after Wayne Gretsky and the disgraced Olympic sprinter Ben Johnson. As WWE's heavyweight champion, he'd taken his role of righteous babyface very much to heart. "In WWE," he said, "I'll always be a hero." But when McMahon made Hart turn face, becoming a heel, and fans began booing him—as they, playing their part in the drama, were supposed to—he took offense.

"I couldn't be a good guy anymore, I couldn't be a bad guy anymore," he said. "I'm stuck with nothing."

Comparing Hart to Hamlet, talk-show pundits in Canada (where it seems everyone takes their wrestling pretty seriously) said that "The Hitman" was caught in a battle of absolute moral values versus moral relativism. But Bret Hart wasn't the only wrestler to have noticed that something was rotten in the state of wrestling. Nearly everyone complained of the backstabbing that went on behind the scenes as they schemed to win favor with the archetypal omnipotent father figure, Vince McMahon. And many were the sons who wanted to take their revenge on the king. "Vince will say he rides his wrestlers just like horses—till they're dead," Hart told me. "Then he cooks 'em and eats 'em. To him, wrestlers are just commodities, like circus animals, to be manipulated and pitted against each other, emotionally and physically."

Except for the cooking and eating part, I didn't understand what Hart was objecting to. Wrestlers had always been commodities; they regarded themselves as such; their being pitted against each other, emotionally and physically, for an audience's amusement was the whole point. But when McMahon saw to it that Hart's tenure would end in defeat, Hart likened the loss to a rape. Backstage after the match, away from the cameras, he spat in the face of the man he'd once thought of as a second father, before knocking him out cold.

All of which was very strange if you thought about it—

and anyone interested in professional wrestling did. Veterans sympathized with Hart wanting to take control of his own destiny. Dealing with transference issues of their own, they certainly didn't mind seeing McMahon get clocked. Still, they had to wonder: What was the big deal about losing a match? It wasn't like any of it was real.

For Bret Hart it was, though.

"Compared to every other wrestler you'll meet, I was rare—I was an artist," he told me within seconds of our sitting down in the cathedral-ceiling living room of his spacious new home outside Calgary. "I was the Robert De Niro of wrestling. If you ever want to see an artist at work, watch my match at Wembley Stadium in front of eighty-two thousand people. I did all the work. I did it without anyone even noticing. What we presented was an epic struggle with our bodies. No good guys. No bad guys. No chair shots. No hair pulling. Just two guys telling a story."

I had difficulty keeping a straight face, yet I realized that Hart was blowing his horn partly to make a larger point about what has happened to the business. Wrestlers like himself and Owen—the real pros of professional wrestling who, night after night, no matter where or with whom they worked, could make a fake fight look legit without hurting anyone— were becoming extinct. "Now we've moved into a whole different era," he said. "You have guys who don't know what they're doing, who just want to be seen, and the only way they know how to do that is brutalizing their bodies. The whole business is a diabolical freak show. And the result is—well, the result is what happened to Owen."

And what happened to Owen was definitive proof, Hart believed, that McMahon was evil. Hart did not say that

McMahon actually plotted the death of his brother. In fact, he made a point of saying that that was *not* what he was saying. What he alleged, rather, was that Vince McMahon had helped create an environment in which someone could die so pointlessly.*

A FLORIDA attorney made a similar argument in defense of a twelve-year-old boy accused of murdering a six-year-old playmate. There was no disputing that Lionel Tate had fatally injured Tiffany Eunick while his mother took a nap. It was attorney Jim Lewis's contention, however, that the boy was only horsing around, imitating the wrestling moves he had seen on television. Lewis's argument got a lot of media attention—as well as a libel suit from WWE—but it did not fly in court. Judge Joel Lazarus would not allow the defense to call professional wrestlers to the stand; he also limited the testimony of a psychiatrist who had interviewed Lionel for over thirty hours. The dismissive attitude of the judge and jury (which found the defendant guilty of first-degree murder and, despite his youth, sentenced him to life in prison without parole) was echoed in the press, as if Lewis had maligned a sacred American institution in a scurrilous "Twinkie" defense.

In fact, Lewis had said what any number of social commentators, from William Bennett to Stanley Fish, have long

---

* A year and a half after Owen Hart's death, WWE settled a wrongful-death suit brought by Hart's wife and his parents with a payment of $18 million.

argued: that popular culture has consequences. But that was a point easier made on op-ed pages and Sunday-morning talk shows than in a criminal court. For, at its essence, the trial was an attempt to make the subtle distinction between objective reality and the subjective interpretation of it. And that raised the quintessential question of professional wrestling: Where did a performance end and reality begin? Wrestling, like almost any theatrical performance, tries to blur those lines. Even after WWE acknowledged the theatricality by calling its shows "sports entertainment," its goal was still to bewitch and bewilder fans into a state of eager credulity.

Dr. Joel Klass, the psychiatrist hired by the defense, testified that Lionel Tate was totally immersed in wrestling culture. "It was his friend, his babysitter, his raison d'être," he told me. He and a psychiatrist called by the prosecution disagreed about whether Lionel believed wrestling was real. But that was never the important question. The question that needed to be answered was whether or not Lionel understood that doing the sort of things that wrestlers did, regardless of whether they were real or make-believe, could be physically harmful.

That a twelve-year-old boy might be confused about this stood to reason. Professional wrestling had to maintain an ambiguous position to the question. On the one hand, it had to appear that the wrestlers really did suffer excruciating injuries in the ring. On the other hand, their injuries ultimately had to seem as harmless as Wile E. Coyote's.

Only they weren't. There was a hard reality to a chair shot; these are standard-issue metal folding chairs, and getting hit in the head with one really hurts. Bones really did get broken. The pain that wrestlers endured was far more real than fans imagined. But it was wrestlers' egos that suffered the most savage abuse. The ritual agonies they enacted in the ring were but a dramatic depiction of the misery so many of them experienced outside it.

A FTER Davey Boy Smith and Diana Hart had taken their fight around the side of the house, I followed Stu Hart up the basement stairs into the kitchen. Bent over double, gnarled with arthritis, his once-enormous trunk now a flabby sack of wasted muscle, the wizened paterfamilias was a far cry from the sadist of wrestling lore. "My back is so stiff," he wheezed. "I'm like an old whore getting off a toilet."

Wherever I traveled, teenage boys were always telling me they planned on going to Stu Hart's infamous dungeon just as soon as they graduated from high school. They hoped to learn the skills of a working pro wrestler and, more importantly, receive the sort of anointing that stars like Mad Dog Vachon, Abdullah the Butcher, Killer Kowalski, Dynamite Kid, and Chris Benoit had been given when they submitted to Stu Hart's famous "stretchings." For sooner or later, anyone who ever entered the dungeon found himself in Stu Hart's ferocious grip. "Bend over here, let me see your neck," he'd say. "I want to show you something."

Before I knew it, this eighty-five-year-old man had *my* neck in the crook of his elbow, his arms locked together, applying pressure to my carotid artery, strangling me.

Fortunately, the telephone rang and as Hart reached to answer it, I squirmed free.

"Hello?" Hart said.

"_____"

"Owen? Owen's not here," he said. "Owen is dead."

"_____"

"Owen was killed in the ring, in Kansas City."

Hart hung up and said nothing about the caller. He wanted to return to our "stretching" exercises. But I got him to talk about his own introduction to submission wrestling as a teenager at the Edmonton YMCA.

"Those boys grabbed me like they owned me and shoved my head up my ass," Hart said in a wheezy whisper that his children did an excellent imitation of. "I had the shit squeezed out of me. I'd say they generally abused me as much as they knew how. Just big goddamned bullies. I didn't mind being mauled like that. I knew I'd get to do it to somebody else someday. I don't want to be boastful, but I did it with all of my boys. I'd put their heads between their knees and give them a little treat. Their tongue would get so thick they couldn't swallow. Their eyes would turn bloodred. They'd black out. I'd drive their foreheads into their belly buttons until they vomited or shit their pants. I made a hobby of that."

Young men traveled far and wide—from Germany, from Turkey, from Russia, from the West Indies—for just this toughening experience. They came, as Davey Boy and Brian Pillman had, hoping for a kind of laying on of hands. In a way, those boys wanted the same thing that I came looking for in the Harts. A sense of moral values, I guess. Or a belief that wrestling could be about something more than image, ego, and opportunism. But it was difficult to see how the Harts could help them now, or restore my illusions; the family was obviously having difficulties of its own. In addition to Owen, another Hart son, Dean, had died in 1990 of Bright's disease, after years of hard living. A thirteen-year-old nephew had died from a flesh-eating infection seemingly triggered by a backyard wrestling accident. The two concussions that Bret had recently suffered in one match would later trigger a stroke. The careers of the erstwhile husbands of Diana, Ellie, and Allison were over. The oldest Hart son, Smith, whom Stu called 'Shead (short for Shithead), was back home living with his parents, refusing to work. Only Bruce and his brother Ross still had a hand in the business, running the wrestling school in the dungeon and trying to revive their father's promotion. They were having a hard time making a go of it, however. Organization was a problem. Talent was a problem. Money was a problem. But the biggest problem was that the kind of wrestling they believed in—wholesome family entertainment, with a respect for the rules, for the referee, for God and Canada—had died, if indeed it ever existed.

"It died the night that Owen died," Allison Hart would tell me. "I hate it, I hate it, I hate it! I hate everything wrestling has become. Bruce and Ross are trying to save something that's gone. I understand what they're trying to do, and I feel for them. But they're tilting at windmills. We've lost it—let it go. If asses like Davey Boy have any part of it, just let it go. . . . You don't want anything to do with it."

STAMPEDE WRESTLING

A FEW HOURS after her fight with Davey Boy, Diana asked if I would drive her home. The police had come while I had been talking to her father, and Diana admitted to throwing a weight-lifting plate at Davey's forty-thousand-dollar BMW, while their twelve-year-old daughter and fourteen-year-old son sat in the backseat. Davey then hurled the weight through the windshield of Diana's brand-new Volkswagen. After we discovered that Davey had

taken her other car as well, we kept driving around town, talking about what a tangled relationship her family had with wrestling, but mostly about her disastrous marriage. It was too bad I didn't have a video camera, she said. Her and Davey's fight would have been a good bit for WWE. "You know, reality TV," she said, not quite joking.

"My dad is always telling me, 'You've got two bee-uuutiful children, you've got to work it out,'" Diana went on, imitating her father. "I want to scream: 'Dad! You've seen it with your own eyes! What do you think of me? That I should just

keep getting treated like this?' I'm just so frustrated. I've become such a sap. I used to be kind of feisty and enthusiastic.
And then one day you try to kill yourself and you end up in the
psychiatric ward."

I said nothing, and after a minute Diana continued.

"Davey was shooting up again. I kept telling everyone,
'Look at him! Look at the track marks on his arms! He can't
even walk!' He'd be out of it for ten hours, and if he did wake
up, it was just to shoot up again. And they kept saying, 'But
he's such a nice guy.' "

One night, going through her husband's coat pockets, looking for some money, Diana found hundreds of pills. She'd had
enough. Swallowing a handful of his Xanaxes, she tried to wake
Davey to show what she was doing. She could have hit him on
the head with a frying pan; he still wouldn't have budged. After
calling 911, she remembers trying to find something to wear
without a lot of buttons, and to have on two matching socks.

"What you need to worry about in that situation," I told
Diana, "is clean underwear."

"And not worry about the socks?"

"The socks aren't important."

"I'll remember that."


I HAD PLANNED on staying nearly a week in Calgary. But
after my interview with Bret the next day, I decided to
leave first thing the next morning. I had seen enough.
Wrestling was supposed to be fun, irreverent, outlandish,
triumphant, festive—and, very often, in places like Viking
Hall, it still was. Yet no other branch of popular culture produced so much misery, and it was starting to depress me.

The rites and rituals of pro wrestling convinced men like Kerry Von Erich and Davey Boy Smith of their natural dominion. They were strong and powerful. They could inflict and incur great pain and suffering. But after years in the business, they held dominion over nothing. At twenty-four, Von Erich had been the second-youngest National Wrestling Alliance champion. Davey Boy Smith had started training at the age of twelve. Coming to Calgary as the poor boy seeking his riches in a New World, he must have felt life was a fairy tale. The eight hale and hearty Hart boys were like brothers to him. Their father had treated him as a son. And to his amazement, the man's youngest and prettiest daughter, a local beauty queen with golden blond hair and the name of a goddess, had fallen in love with him.

Neither he nor Von Erich lived happily ever after, however. Von Erich dropped down the card as he failed to make show dates and court appointments until, one by one, the major promotions dropped him altogether. Davey Boy Smith's employers had discarded him, too. After Owen Hart's death, Smith thought McMahon might take him back into the fold. But with his ongoing drug addiction, WWE would have nothing to do with him. His wife then left him for another wrestler. And later, after taking up with his brother-in-law Bruce's wife, he had become a pariah to his adopted family.

"Davey has always been a follower," Bret Hart told me, meaning that Smith was now following a long line of self-destructive wrestlers who crashed cars, abandoned families, beat their wives, shot at police, missed shows, and passed out in the ring, in the locker room, and in airplanes, burning bridges everywhere they went. The false selves they created in defense of the miserable desolation they felt within had, like Dr. Frankenstein's monster, gone on a narcissistic rampage.

The one thing that had saved these men in the past, their physical strength, was of absolutely no use to them now.

I visited Bret on the longest day of the year. At 9:30 P.M., the sun peaked under a blanket of dark clouds and backlit a column of rain as a spectacular storm tumbled over the Rockies to the west. We realized that I should get a move on before the deluge. But before I left, Bret brought me downstairs to his personal hall of fame. I don't think he was trying to show off. Rather, he seemed to want to step back and get perspective on where wrestling had taken him and what had become of the business. Inevitably, his ruminations brought him back to his childhood and the confusion he felt watching his father manage a struggling promotion.

"Stampede Wrestling didn't have the flash and flamboyance," he said as we studied dozens of pictures and wrestling-magazine covers chronicling his career. "It was a territory that lived and died by its reality. As a kid, I didn't always understand that, but I knew something was up. I'd see a guy break my father's arm. The next day, he'd come up to the house to get his check and my mom would pat him on the back. After a while I realized that, even though it was all just a show, when it's done right there could be a sincerity. That's why I got into it. It's not real, though. What's real is Owen's death, and yet even that was made into a work. People were thinking 'What's the catch?' That's wrestling in a nutshell."

Hart stopped himself to point to pictures of others who had died, usually as a result of their own misadventures. "This guy, he's dead," he said. "Here's another one. And another one. And this guy, he's a big downer junkie; with him, it's only a matter of time." He paused, taking in all the pictures on the wall. "You could throw a dart and say who's next. The next tragedy is tomorrow. I could name at least fifteen guys who are huge painkiller addicts."

"I hate to say this," I said, interrupting, "but your sister Diana is married to a dead man, too."

"Yeah," Hart nodded, without emotion. "Davey Boy is probably one of the next to go."

Well, not the next—at least twenty other wrestlers would check out in the next two years, all before the age of forty-five—but three years after the death of his brother-in-law, Davey Boy Smith did die of a heart attack, brought on by years of drug abuse. He was thirty-eight.

Von Erich had taken his own life ten years earlier, shooting himself in the heart the day before he was scheduled to work a rinky-dink indie match with a wrestler who called himself The Angel of Death.

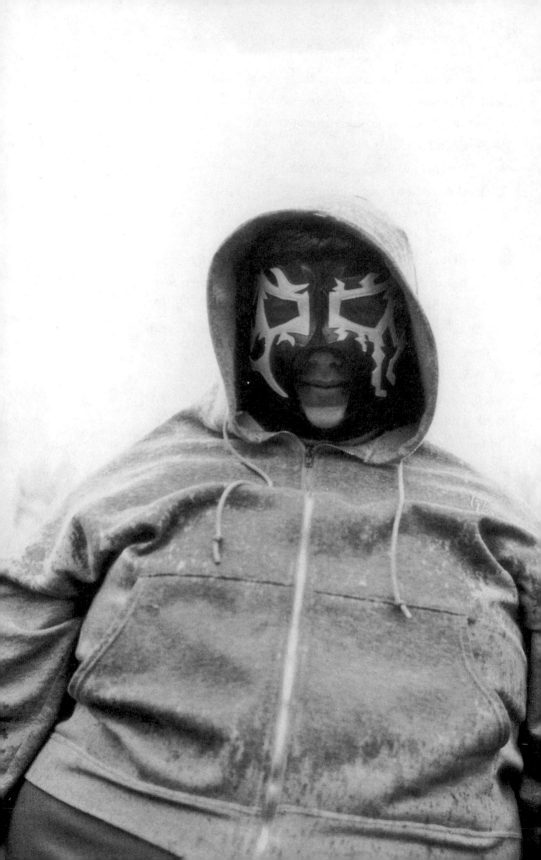

# CHAPTER TWELVE

WE ARE ALL IN THE GUTTER, BUT SOME OF US
ARE LOOKING AT THE STARS.

—OSCAR WILDE

A T THE END of *Requiem for a Heavyweight*, the washed-up old boxer Mountain Rivera is given one last piece of advice before he steps in the wrestling ring: "Don't get carried away."

If Rivera was listening, it seems nobody else was. In the years since that movie's release, the whole country seems to have gotten carried away with the spectacle of image and status and celebrity, to the point where nobody could tell the exemplary from the execrable. Anyone for whom honesty and sincerity still mattered, or who wasn't capable of going along with hokum and humbug, seemed deficient somehow, retarded in his cultural development. On this, Daniel Boorstin was way ahead of everyone. Yet I doubt even he could have predicted that the people of Minnesota would elect a professional wrestler their governor, or that another wrestler (The Rock, who had never voted, who in WWE shows referred to women as "poontang pie") would be invited to speak at the 2000 Republican presidential convention, helping to nominate a man who, as president, would play dress-up as a fighter pilot and would later support a bodybuilder's successful run for the governorship of California.

It was hard to know what to make of it all. Was the political ascendance of professional posers an expression of populist sentiment? Or had we entered a period of fin de siècle decadence? Was everyone now a performance artist? If so, perhaps it was not surprising that the distinction between entertainment and reality (or what wrestlers call a "work" and a "shoot") would become so hazy that a man's death was taken as just another performance. If "life itself is a dramatically enacted thing," as sociologist Erving Goffman writes in *The Presentation of Self in Everyday Life*, it seemed that in the warped world of professional wrestling, so, too, was death.

To my mind, the tragedies of pro wrestling merely pointed up the calamities that were bound to occur when a culture got caught up in its own spectacular illusions.

In the weeks after September 11, 2001, the country appeared to have snapped out of that daze. For a while there, everybody seemed content just to be themselves, without regard to image or status, and to appreciate others just as they were. Curious to see if the harrowing but also heroic images of recent events hadn't altered the fantasies around which wrestling revolved, I went to WWE's twenty-five-million-dollar theme restaurant in Times Square about a week after the attacks. The restaurant was on the same itinerary for tourists as Planet Hollywood and the Hard Rock Cafe, and the food was nearly as bad. But in order to keep abreast of wrestling developments, I had made a point of regularly paying the five-dollar cover on Monday nights, when *Raw*, the highest-rated show on cable television, aired. (Let me repeat that: WWE charged fans, and we happily paid, to watch TV.) Most Mondays a line formed outside the building, with velvet ropes and burly bouncers creating a sense of exclusivity. Not surprisingly, that was not the case on this night, but once you went downstairs to a basement dining room abuzz with the familiar histrionics on regular and super-large-screen TVs, you felt as if you had gone back in time. I imagine that, for many fans, watching wrestlers act out their preposterous egoism was a comforting escape from a frightening reality. For some, though, it seemed to be much more than that. It seemed, that is, a way of pledging allegiance to everything wrestling stood for. One guy in his mid-twenties told me ashamedly that he had fled the city in a panic the morning of the attacks; now, he said, he was ready to fight back. How? By watching wrestling. By eating at a wrestling-themed restaurant.

Supposedly, 9/11 reminded the country of what real heroism meant. Pat Tillman, a professional football player, stopped playing a warrior on the field and became a real one in Iraq and Afghanistan, where he was killed in combat. But no other men or women of prominence followed his example of selfless service. Only one member of Congress had a son or daughter serving in the region. Despite the initial gung-ho patriotism and the bestselling paeans to the "greatest generation" of

World War II, the armed forces saw no surge of enlistments (indeed, they would have trouble meeting their recruitment targets). Neither did police and fire departments. "There's a difference between interest and action," said a Chicago advertising director who helped create the U.S. Army's new "Army of one" campaign to replace its "Be all you can be" slogan. The theme of the short-lived campaign identified the problem—getting what Secretary of the Army Louis Caldera called a "me-now" generation to embrace a life of self-sacrifice and teamwork—but it also seemed to exacerbate it.

What was the point of bravery if it didn't have an audience? Why bother being a man of action when you could become an action figure instead?

THE LONGER Matt (Wifebeater) Prince stayed in the business, the more he wrestled with that very question.

"A way to be more than average"—that, Prince said when we first met at a Combat Zone Wrestling show in Philadelphia, was what he'd been searching for. At the time, wrestling in barbed wire, in glass, on thumbtacks, and amid explosives seemed a good way to achieve that distinction. Although he'd previously had a dim view of pro wrestling, after his first indie show he became convinced that lacerating his chest and back with a weed whacker did in fact distinguish him from the average person. As he put it: "It's all about not being a little bitch." But after a while, he began to realize that was *not* what the weed whacker was all about. Indeed, it occurred to him that the abuse he subjected himself to had really been about massive insecurity.

"It's like what Billy Corgan of the band Smashing Pumpkins said: 'If I ever got the love I needed as a kid, I wouldn't need it from millions of people when I'm onstage,' " Prince told me months later. "I think that's true of wrestlers, too. It's a bunch of guys who badly, badly want to be liked. You're constantly bombarded with celebrities, and you feel you have to keep up with that—like, unless you're a celebrity, you're nobody. It's like what Andy Warhol said—'In the future, everybody gets to be famous for fifteen minutes.' That's almost true now, with shows like *Real World*. It feels like that's the only way to be really alive. And I'm lucky. I've experienced more fame than most people. I've had my own baseball card, my own T-shirts. I can show people my action figure . . ."

"I take it that's not a euphemism," I said.

Prince laughed.

"Wrestling *is* a good way to get pussy," he said. "Like the caveman probably figured out that coming home all tired and cut up from fighting the woolly mammoth brought out the motherly nursing thing in cavewoman. Sympathy is one of the most appealing things to get from someone. I love getting sympathy. It's great. I think: 'I'll fuck myself up, maybe that'll get the sympathy I really want.' "

We had been talking after one of Wifebeater's epic death matches, as Prince waited for paramedics to stitch up the soft underside of his arm, where a snag of barbed wire had ripped away the flesh. He would not need any stitches on his back; scar tissue covered virtually all of it, like armor. But this was to be Prince's last match. He had decided to walk away from wrestling and his fame. He had enrolled in a truck-driving school, to learn how to manage eighteen-wheelers in the hairiest city traffic. Aside from the money he would make—

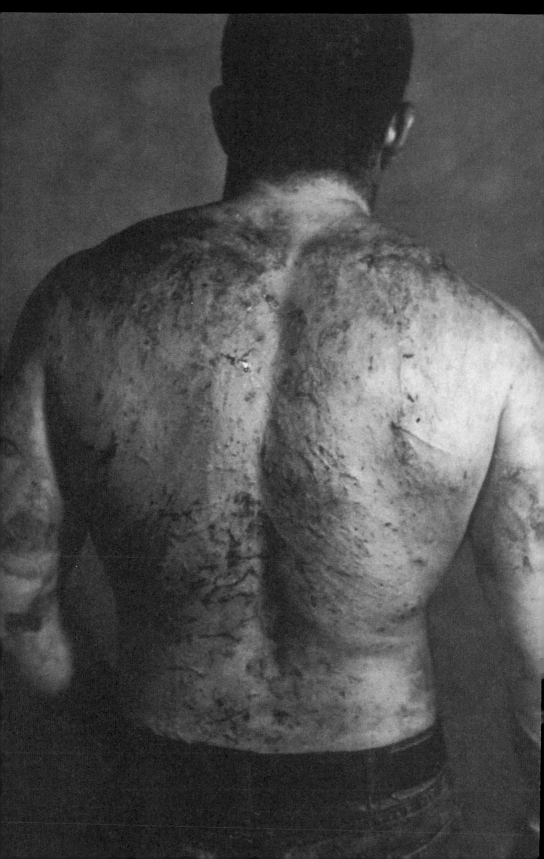

much better than the couple of hundred dollars he made wrestling once a week, tops—the job appealed to his temperament. "Another manly job," he said.

Matt Burns, aka Nick Mondo, was in line to take Wifebeater's place as the hardcore icon on the Combat Zone roster. But a few weeks later, Burns told me that he, too, was hoping to quit soon. He'd had his sights set on one particular goal, and it looked like he was about to achieve it: his own action figure. "All of the injuries and all the hardships will have been worth it," he said. "To me it's almost like being immortalized—your actual body! It's something no one can ever take away from you. If someone asks, 'Were you good?' I can say, 'Well, look, I had an action figure made!' "

In the future, maybe everyone will have his own action figure. Until then, I was always relieved whenever a young wrestler like Matt Prince or Matt Burns called it quits. I had met and heard about too many men who lived in a fantasy world blurred beyond all recognition by drinking, drugs, their own delusions, and the inanities of the culture. "Eventually the confusion sets in," Roddy Piper told me. "All you've ever done is create an illusion. And all you've got to show for it are some smelly tights, which you hang over the lamp in your hotel room to dry for the next day. Sure, there are fans all around you, like you're important. But inside, you ain't nothing but a piece of shit."

And yet, just minutes before, Piper had said: "Wrestling saved my life. Without it, I don't know where I'd be."

The calculus was tricky. The one wrestler who seemed to have it all figured out was Dwayne Johnson, and he wasn't

OPPOSITE: WIFEBEATER

long for the business. The others—even the smart wrestlers, the ones who knew the difference between a work and a shoot—often remained lost in the funhouse decades after entering the ring, still trying to find themselves.

T HE DISILLUSIONMENT of fans was a less encouraging development, since it meant that something they had been able to call their own, that they had actively created, had become just another alienated commercial experience. It would be a fan calling himself Black Venom who brought home to me the wonderful immediacy of live hardcore indie wrestling. We met at an ECW show in Los Angeles. He had been drinking since nine-thirty that morning—eight bloody marys, a twelve-pack of beer, and he wasn't sure how many shots of Jack Daniel's. Toward the end of the show, on a curious whim, he decided to vomit on a wrestler. "A little heave is all, not a full-blown puke," he explained. "But next thing I know, they're all over me! All of them!"

"All of them?" I asked.

"A bunch of them."

"The wrestlers? Not the security guys?"

"I don't know," he said. "It was a fucked-up situation. They weren't listening to me. I'm a nobody. But fuck them! Once I start making money . . . forget about it."

"Did you fight back?" I asked.

"I fucking should have. I know the moves. I can take a chair shot. I'd be a wrestler if I could."

"Why can't you?"

"I don't want to get into that right now."

I had a flight to catch and was running late, so I asked Black Venom if he wanted to take a drive to the airport. With no one else to throw up on, and with a flight of his own much later that night, he figured what the hell.

"It's like this," he said as we got in my rental car. "I can live vicariously through their violence without going out and beating myself up."

"But, in effect, that's just what you did," I said.

"Fucking-A! I'm going to hire a fucking lawyer! They said I puked on Sandman, but that's bullshit. I wouldn't do that to Sandman."

"Why wouldn't you puke on Sandman?"

"Because he's fucking Sandman, that's why! The guy is awesome!"

"The guy who drinks beer and hits people with that thing?"

"A Singapore whipping cane! The dude is fuckin' awesome!"

"The other guys you *would* puke on, though?"

"This is my thing. I go to shows and get in fights. If I really wanted to be evicted, I would have fucking shit on them, I would have pissed on them. I wouldn't have cared. Plus, today's my birthday."

Needless to say, birthday or no birthday, this was not something a civilized culture was supposed to encourage. But I had to hand it to Black Venom: if he was disgusted with the superior attitudes of athletes and actors and musicians and politicians and professional wrestlers—of all the people whose lot in life seemed so much better than his own—he had made his point.

At bottom, probably all fans of popular culture have a deeply ambivalent relationship with their objects of fascination. Wrestling fans were fortunate, though. Cheering this wrestler and jeering that one, vacillating wildly between adoration and disdain, they had the opportunity to actively express their profound ambivalence about celebrity culture. Although a fan like Urial Yakobov would often say that being famous didn't mean you were better than anyone else ("This is America! It's a democracy! Everybody is equal!"), to him it was self-evident that wrestlers, like all celebrities, deserved their higher order of existence. "Why shouldn't they think they're better?" he asked. "They're on TV." The statement was not meant to be sarcastic. But in his very next breath Urial reversed himself. "It's not them, it's the fans who are pissing their pants who make them think they're better," he explained. "It's like how girls are. If you're all up their ass, they're going to think they're all that. Why? Because of us moron guys running after them, degrading ourselves."

I think we are all as vexed by the spectacle of modern fame as Urial is. We're all morons, pissing our pants. The difference is, wrestling fans have found a place where they can give full voice to their profound ambivalence. The rest of us just go along with the media's obsessions, ignoring or disguising our resentments. We learn to read *People* and *Us* ironically. When we watch the Academy Awards, we only dish about the dresses. We don't vomit on them.

According to Mikhail Bakhtin, it was the crude, rude, and fabulously lewd culture of the carnival that expressed the true spirit of the Middle Ages. The great literature of the time, from Chaucer to Cervantes to Rabelais to Shakespeare, reeks of the

subversive sensibility. Usually, though, we are able to appreciate the eloquence of vulgarity and debauchery only in hind-
sight, from a distance of centuries, while dismissing today's
forms of tomfoolery as nothing more than the asinine work of
adolescent minds. There's good reason for that. The truth is,
popular culture often *is* imbecilic and immature. But that's not
all it is. It is also defiant, hopeful, liberating, and unifying.

For me, it was one thing to read that bawdy humor "frees
human consciousness," as Bakhtin writes, or that nothing
counters "the mockeries of the world" like laughter, as
Bonaventura says. It's quite another to be at a wrestling show
where hundreds of metal folding chairs are flying through the
air and to realize you are one of the people throwing them. For
a funny thing had happened: as the teenage boys I met on
Urial's bus trips were developing a connoisseur's appercep-
tion for the more artful forms of "scientific" wrestling, my
own tastes evolved in the other direction. I had been liberated
from some of my priggish prejudices. I discovered what
wrestling's critics overlooked, and what even many of the
wrestlers themselves had forgotten—that at its best, its
freest, wrestling was pure play. Violent play, to be sure; play
that used puerile humor to deflect a potent mishmash of aggressive and affectionate impulses. But genuine hostility seldom intruded on the roughhousing. As far as I was concerned,
the more barbaric the show the better.

Unfortunately, I had cottoned to something just as it was
disappearing.

D ESPITE an earlier vow, one day Urial Yakobov phoned and announced that he was done with wrestling. "Urial the fucking mark" is how he referred to himself. "I don't care about this shit anymore. My days of supporting these guys are over. They can go fuck themselves. Before, wrestling was my life. Everything I did was wrestling. Everything I read. Everything I talked about. Everybody I knew—it was wrestling. But I'm older now. My mind is starting to work a little better. Now I'm saying to myself, 'Get a life!' "

Eventually I understood what was going on: Urial's sentimental education had entered a new phase. Ostensibly, he and I got together so I could interview him about wrestling. More often than not, we would talk about an even more fascinating and confounding subject: girls. One night, for instance, he called to say that he had met a girl so heartbreakingly beautiful he just had to cry. Compared to that, I agreed—wrestling *could* seem pretty inconsequential.

So I thought he wouldn't mind hearing about the run-in that his once-beloved Extreme Championship Wrestling had had with Rob Zicari's crew at the Olympic Auditorium in Los Angeles. Witnessing the fracas, I had taken the episode to be an elaborate work meant to generate a little heat for the benefit of both companies, and I figured aficionados would enjoy figuring out how it had been engineered. In fact, though, the stunt deeply offended most fans, Urial chief among them.

"Don't you understand?" he told me back in New York. "This business is all about respect! Those guys from XPW [Zicari's company] were cursing, shouting obscenties, calling the ECW wrestlers names!"

"Cursing? Shouting obscenities . . . ?" I said.

URIAL YAKOBOV—ALL GROWN UP

"Look," he said, "when I first started with ECW, they sucked big time. But I worked my ass off on these bus trips, and a lot of times I lost money. But I believed in ECW. I loved ECW. It's something that's part of me. And these morons . . ."

So, upon reflection, Urial decided that his period of dismay had been a test of faith. As he now explained: "It's not loyalty; it's love. It's like fighting with your parents. You still love them. You'll always love them."

**B**UT IT WAS not to last. A few months after Paul Heyman proclaimed, "We're kicking ass," it had become clear that the only asses getting kicked were those working or cheering for ECW. Like the old territorial federations, his company had been faring decently so long as its ambitions remained modest, never straying outside New York, New Jersey, and Pennsylvania. But once it landed a cable television deal on TNN (then called The Nashville Network, now called Spike TV), Heyman had to pay the fiddler, taking the show on the road to sustain a national audience. And with WWE and WCW raiding his locker room, he also had to pay the available talent far more than he could afford. Attentive fans, who monitored developments in the wrestling market as closely as Wall Street investors, heard that Heyman had canceled shows and bounced checks. And when the company lost its television contract, wrestlers who had not been properly paid in months began walking; others stayed because—well, where else could they go? Most weren't ready for prime time, and never would be, lacking the charisma and the holy shit! physicality capable of reaching an audience of millions. They were maybe a little small, or a little pudgy, or too naturally self-effacing. A few were simply drug-addicted thugs who did not belong in anyone's living room.

Laid up after a motorcycle accident, I had missed months of live wrestling. Reading a lot during that time, I noticed that hardly a day went by that a newspaper or magazine didn't liken the squabbles in politics or business or academia or law (or whatever) to pro wrestling. Wrestling seemed the perfect metaphor for the way Americans settled their differences. Yet these journalists were talking about the antics in the ring. To me, professional wrestling was something else—it was the unruly camaraderie and giddy rejection of social decencies. And, to my surprise, I found myself missing it, missing the lived experience, the freedom of misbehaving, of losing myself in a crowd gone berserk. At the time, I could not have put a finger on any of this. But when Urial called a few days before Christmas and insisted that, to hell with my injuries, I had better come to an Elks Lodge on Queens Boulevard, that it was likely to be ECW's last show in New York, perhaps its last ever, I obediently hobbled out on an icy winter night.

With its giant chandeliers and coffered ceiling, the lodge was a fancy banquet hall from a bygone era. The Elks had decamped, and the lodge, in serious disrepair, was in the process of being taken over by a religious cult that did not abide the head-bashing violence of hardcore wrestling. It occurred to me, though, as we waited for the show to begin, that for all their obvious philosophical differences, wrestling fans, religious cultists, and a fraternal service organization probably all shared the sentiments emblazoned on the four balcony walls above the ring:

## CHARITY
## JUSTICE
## BROTHERLY LOVE
## FIDELITY

The room sat only three hundred spectators, but Heyman squeezed in twice as many, with fans bellying up to the ring, close enough to hear the wrestlers guiding one another through their choreography in gentle whispers. Urial had paid sixty dollars for a ringside seat. I paid ten and stood only ten feet behind him. To my right was a boy with Down's syndrome; to my left a fat, prematurely bald teenage boy in a yellow-and-black zigzaggy Charlie Brown T-shirt; next to him a Sikh boy wearing a turban. The four of us stood atop an upright piano shoved into a corner. From there, we could easily see over the heads of the fans in front of us but had to crouch to see under the low balcony.

Most of the show I didn't need to watch, having seen the skits countless times before. The wrestlers swaggered into the ring, tussled, punched, kicked, danced, bounced off ropes, hit one another with chairs, and disregarded the referee. What else is there? Yet everyone agreed it was an extraordinary night. Taking off his snakeskin jacket, Joel Gertner read one of his bawdy poems and rubbed his flabby man-breasts in Dawn Marie's face. Tommy Dreamer pulled down his sweatpants and rubbed his jiggly rear end in the face of C. W. Anderson. Sandman spewed beer from the balcony, making like he was masturbating. Justin Credible and Kid Kash tickled each other's hands. When a girl in the audience would not expose her breasts, several fat boys flaunted theirs. And for over three hours, the entire congregation kept up a nonstop litany of chants, from the usual "Suck His Dick" and "On Your Knees" to "Wel-Come Back," "Please Don't Go," and what sounded like "L-U-V."

Even if I hadn't heard that last chant correctly, the lodge did seem bathed in an atmosphere of complete and unconditional love. A kind of religious love, I mean—a feeling of oneness and warmth, a sense of being absorbed into something greater than one's own self.

In a business of selfish free agents and no-account scoundrels, ECW had maintained an amazing feeling of solidarity for a remarkable eight-year run. And tonight its wrestlers would have a hard time disguising their sadness that it would soon end and they'd each be left to fend for themselves. This being professional wrestling, they couldn't openly express their fondness for one another; affection first had to pass through a sieve of abuse. The boys in the audience joined in, too, cheerfully raining epithets down from the balcony, particularly on the Dudley Boyz, a tag team that had started at ECW, establishing a reputation for crashing through particleboard tables before going on to greater glories, crashing through particleboard tables at WWE. "The guys who have come through here are now at the top of the motherfucking world," Paul Heyman said, making a rare appearance in the ring. "In ECW, boys became men, and men became heroes. In the WWE, heroes became legends and legends became gods. If it weren't for ECW, the Dudley Boyz wouldn't be the hardcore gods they are. What makes them superstars is that they never forget the work ethic they learned in a building like this, performing for people like you."

The speech was absurd. The Dudley Boyz were not gods, legends, heroes, or even men. They were overgrown boys, still playing games of make-believe. But I wasn't rolling my eyes now. Behind the bombast, Heyman had said something important about feeling connected to a rare experience, and I, in my own grudging and critical way, had been part of it.

The show had gone on for hours, well past midnight, and still nobody wanted to leave. Wrestling matches often end in the melee of a battle royal, with the entire locker room piling into the ring for one last giddy free-for-all. But tonight they did not even bother. Wrestlers who usually guarded the conceit of their supposed animosity now hugged and kissed one another. It was there all along—the intimacy. As all art is said to aspire to the condition of music, all wrestling aspires to the condition of brotherly love.

And then it was over. The Elks Lodge exhaled hundreds of anxious teenage boys into the cold night, leaving a sweltering room heavy with the stench of perspiration and frustrated aspirations. Urial remained. He had got to the lodge at ten in the morning, running errands, setting up chairs, assembling the ring, hoisting loudspeakers, and distributing promotional flyers around the city, thinking that just this once, in appreciation for all he'd contributed, Heyman's lackeys might let him backstage. They didn't, but he wasn't angry. He would stay another three hours, breaking down the ring, putting away the chairs, not getting paid a penny for his efforts.

For the moment, though, he just stood by himself, staring into the empty ring. He didn't even try to hide the tears streaming down his face.

PAUL HEYMAN did throw in the towel after the Elks Lodge show. Filing for bankruptcy, he went to work for WWE, taking a few of his wrestlers with him. Others landed jobs with WCW. That company was losing money to the tune of $80 million a year, however, and soon went out of business, as well. "I'm going to take over the world," Vince McMahon had declared twenty years earlier. Now, it seemed, he had. But without the heat of head-to-head competition and the gonzo authenticity of ECW energizing the business, his ratings began to sag. Soon the company closed shop on its Times Square restaurant and ditched its grandiose plans for theme parks, hotels, television dramas, and its own television station.

Urial Yakobov again lost interest in wrestling, this time for good. He began dating a religious girl, and threw himself into Orthodox Judaism with as much fervor as he'd had for hardcore professional wrestling. Now when we got together, it had to be at kosher restaurants. And we were no longer permitted to talk about wrestling. He said he was disgusted to have been associated with other fans. "I have one image in my head: a guy who has never kissed a girl," he said. "Well, I was that guy. I was like a loser, and it doesn't make me feel good."

I never for a second thought that the satisfaction Urial and his friends got from wrestling disgraced or dishonored them. In fact, I envied their unabashed enthusiasm. I wished more of us could find as much pure joy in our culture as they found in pro wrestling. As for the wrestlers, though I feared for their future, the truth is that I was heartened to know that guys like Michael Thornton and James Maritato and Oren Hawxhurst were still pursuing their dreams.

In Hawxhurst's case, the future had looked promising for a while. Rob Zicari tried to take over where ECW had left off, leaving Los Angeles to run shows out of Viking Hall, and Hawxhurst appeared on the verge of becoming one of XPW's stars. But then things got messy for Extreme Associates. For starters, The Messiah had an affair with Zicari's porn-star wife, and soon thereafter a couple of thugs burst into his apartment and tried chopping off his genitals with a bolt cutter. In that, they did not succeed; however, they did make off with his right thumb. Despite rumors, police never implicated

Zicari in the attack. But then John Ashcroft and the United States Justice Department charged Zicari and his wife with obscenity and that was it for XPW. Kevin Kleinrock, who himself had married a former porn star and become a father, left wrestling to start his own adult entertainment company. (Porn was a far saner, more businesslike business, he said.) The Messiah found work with Combat Zone Wrestling, but never quite managed to cash in on the cachet of his missing thumb.

Sandman likewise struggled, with wrestling and alcohol, but soon got back together with his wife. Michael Thornton found his professional prospects to be as limited as his mentor Roland Alexander predicted. But after finishing at the top of his semipro class, he continued on at the school as a kind of graduate assistant, teaching others. Perseverance also paid off for James Maritato, who got called up to WWE, where he became exactly what he wanted to be—a reliable mid-card jobber, an old-school worker, going by the name Little Nunzio. Hawxhurst also got a one-night tryout with WWE, wrestling a dark (nontelevised) match when *Raw* came to his hometown of New Orleans. Although his father and mother did not come to watch, just about everyone else he knew did, including his estranged wife and his four-year-old son, Perry. "Daddy," Perry had said after his match, crying, "I'm so proud of you!" At that moment, the debt of Oren's own father's neglect seemed to have been repaid, with interest.

Since we'd first met in Philadelphia, Hawxhurst had abandoned the skinhead look, adopting one hairdo after another. He had a perm now, specifically modeled after Justin Timberlake's, and he hoped that he had finally found a look that would lead to success—a success he wanted to believe he was entitled to. "I deserve it a lot more than most of the guys,"

 OREN HAWXHURST

he complained. Nothing really came of the tryout, though. Soon Hawxhurst was back to driving thousands of miles to work for promotions that nobody had ever heard of. I worried that if Hawxhurst ever did make it to the big time, the love and approval he so desperately longed for would always seem just beyond his reach. Still, it was important to me that Oren Hawxhurst keep chasing after all the magnificent promises that a career in professional wrestling symbolized to him. No, it was not my idea of success, but that didn't matter. All that really did matter was his keeping a dream, any dream, alive.

So that night months earlier, as we were driving back home to New Orleans from the show in Cornelia, Georgia, I didn't tell Oren what I thought of the show a few hours earlier. It had taken place in a kind of barn on a country road, in front of no more than fifty people. To his cousin Timmy, most of those fans looked to have something chromosomally wrong with them, and I had to agree. Hawxhurst performed in a tag-team match with and against three friends he had made while working for XPW. For this they each got paid exactly nothing. In fact, nobody got paid. But Hawxhurst didn't complain. Despite how late it was, well after midnight, he must have called a half-dozen friends, telling them how much the crowd loved him, how spectacularly he had gotten over. I imagined the other twenty guys on the card making a similar round of phone calls. The next day, Hawxhurst would be back at work, crawling underneath houses, trying to figure out why others, for whom wrestling obviously didn't mean nearly as much as it did for him, had found success and he hadn't.

For the moment, though, the future seemed to rise smoothly into stardom, just beyond our headlights.

# NOTES

## INTRODUCTION: DEMENTIA AMERICANA

1   *"The entire spectacle is before us":* Joseph Campbell, *The Hero with a Thousand Faces,* p. 256.

2   Bill Zehme describes Andy Kaufman's adventures in professional wrestling in *Lost in the Fun House: The Life and Mind of Andy Kaufman* (New York: Delta, 1999).

3   Michael Lewis tells the story of the fifteen-year-old day-trader Jonathan Lebed in *Next: The Future Just Happened* (New York: Norton, 2001).

4   *"the best that man has thought and known":* Matthew Arnold, "Sweetness and Light," *Culture and Anarchy* (London: Cambridge University Press, 1961), p. 70.

4   *"to invent a vocabulary and a language":* Lewis Mumford, *Art and Technics,* p. 32.

5   *"wrestling gives 'concrete and public form' ":* Ibid. p. 32.

## CHAPTER ONE: SLOUCHING TOWARD BETHLEHEM

7   *"our whole life is like a play":* Ben Jonson, "Timber, or Discoveries Made Upon Men and Matter" (1641).

8    *a story that we, too, were telling ourselves about ourselves:* I have taken this locution from Clifford Geertz's essay on the Balinese cockfight: "Deep Play," *The Interpretation of Cultures,* p. 121.

8    *the industry was making more than $450 million a year:* USA *Today* (September 6, 2001). Or at least WWE was making money, despite the failure of its professional football league. After losing $65 million in 2000, WCW would close shop in April 2001. World Wrestling Entertainment, on the other hand, maintained several revenue streams: some 200 live events a year, with an average attendance of 9,000 per show (*Wrestling Observer Newsletter,* April 8, 2002); cable television, reaching 22 million viewers a week; pay-per-view broadcasts, with 6.8 million buys for the year; licensing, with $650 million in sales of branded merchandise; book publishing, in which three wrestlers' memoirs had already reached the *New York Times* bestseller list; magazine publishing; and international broadcasts in more than a hundred countries (WWE Corporate Highlights).

8    *the largest indoor gathering in the history of the human race: Current Biography Yearbook 1999,* p. 382.

9    *"We are the voice of the people":* Something Linda McMahon told me in a January 2001 interview at WWE corporate headquarters in Stamford, Connecticut.

12    *Sports Illustrated,* December 13, 1993.

16    *football hooligans . . . attacking anything that represented civilized society:* Bill Buford describes that culture in *Among the Thugs.*

17    *"the 'boys-will-be-boys' kind of boy":* Physical Culture, 1902.

17    *"pale, narrow-chested, hunched up, miserable specimens":* Buford uses the Robert Baden-Powell quotation, from *Scouting for Boys* (1908), as an epigraph.

18    Christina Hoff Sommers discusses "The Harvard Project on Women's Psychology, Boys' Development and the Culture of Manhood" in *The War Against Boys,* pp. 124–32. The study

was published by Carol Gilligan as "The Centrality of Relationships in Human Development: A Puzzle, Some Evidence, and a Theory," in *Development and Vulnerability in Close Relationships,* eds. Gil Noam and Kurt Fischer (Mahwah, N.J.: Erlbaum, 1996).

18   *"The boys in Littleton are the tip of the iceberg":* William Pollack quoted in Sarah Glazer's "Boys' Emotional Needs: Is Growing Up Tougher for Boys Than Girls?" *Congressional Quarterly Researcher,* June 18, 1999, p. 523.

21   *there are "I-quit" matches, battles royal, bunkhouse brawls:* Captain Lou Albano and Bert Randolph Sugar's *The Complete Idiot's Guide to Pro Wrestling* is an excellent primer in wrestling terminology and, in general, an instructive book.

22   *Vince McMahon's publicly traded $1 billion WWE:* That is roughly what the stock market valued the company at when it went public in October 1999; its stock has since fallen significantly.

25   *someone had given the dorky, insecure boys permission to openly enjoy wrestling:* Malcolm Gladwell doesn't write about professional wrestling in *The Tipping Point: How Little Things Can Make a Big Difference* (Boston: Little, Brown, 2000), but he might well have since its sudden popularity in the late 1990s (and also its sudden decline) had all the features of the other social epidemics he examines. My idea that the enthusiasm of certain fans like Urial Yakobov could be literally contagious came from Gladwell's fascinating book. Elias Canetti makes a similar observation in *Crowds and Power,* speaking of those around whom crowds crystallize.

CHAPTER TWO: ORIGINS OF A SPECIES

31   *"The farther one gets from folly":* Erasmus, *The Praise of Folly,* p. 16.

31   Nat Fleisher's *From Milo to Londos* surveys Western civilization's affinity for wrestling but is especially interested in late-nineteenth- and early-twentieth-century American figures

such as William Muldoon, Frank Gotch, Strangler Lewis, and Jim Londos.

31    *"Wrestling, in a noble, manly forbearing and human practice"*: Ibid., p. 11.

32    UCLA drama professor Michael Hackett (no relation) provided useful background on the history and evolution of theater.

33    Walter "Cross-buttocker" Armstrong complains about the "equivocal conduct" of professional wrestlers in *Wrestling* (New York: Frederick. A. Stokes, 1890), pp. xiii, xi.

33    Lou Thesz retails stories about Fred Grubmier and Chief Chewacki in *Hooker,* pp. 37–38, 197–98.

33    *"truly handsome, kind and scholarly"*: Fleischer, p. 31.

33    *the "shapely and grand" Muldoon*: Theodore Dreiser, "Culhane, the Solid Man," *Twelve Men* (New York: Boni and Liveright, 1919), p. 137.

34    *"typified exactly what an artist would seek to portray"*: Fleischer, p. 135.

34    *"Gotch turned a scornful face"*: Ibid., p. 138.

34    *"like trying to grip a well-buttered eel"*: Ibid., p. 103.

34    *"achieved that perfect poise"*: Ibid., p. 123.

35    *"the greatest fiasco ever perpetrated"*: Marcus Griffin, *Fall Guys,* p. 140.

35    Griffin and Fleisher both chronicle the varied careers of Jack Curley, Toots Mondt, Paul Bowser, Jack Pfefer, et al.

35    *"not an inspiring spectacle"*: A. J. Liebling, "The Opera-House Slugger," *The New Yorker,* October 30, 1937.

36    Along with Griffin and Thesz, Joe Jares writes extensively about the creativity and the extracurricular activities of wrestling promoters in *Whatever Happened to Gorgeous George?*

37   *Born Christopher Theophelus in Argos, Greece:* Joel Sayre profiled Jim Londos for *The New Yorker,* "The Pullman Theseus," March 5, 1932. Fleischer's chronicle of this period also provides biographical background on Londos, pp. 236–303.

37   *"fellows who could hold their own":* Griffin, p. 201.

37   Fleischer, Griffin, and *The New Yorker* all report on the crowds Londos drew in New York.

37   *"who we know we can exploit properly":* Griffin, p. 201.

37   *"What a man!":* Joel Sayre, *The New Yorker,* March 5, 1932.

38   *"I'm the big drawing card":* Griffin, p. 149.

38   *"I'm through and what are you going to do about it?":* Ibid., p. 149.

38   *"Them thiefs is stealin' ":* Ibid., p. 165.

39   *"the titular bouts of the past were far more interesting":* Fleischer, p. 236.

39   *"It was a period of re-evaluation":* Liebling, "From Sarah Bernhardt to Yukon Eric," *The New Yorker,* November 13, 1954.

39   *"I am very proud of some of my monstrosities":* Colliers, October 22, 1938.

39   *"A swerve a day keeps the blues away":* Jares, *Whatever Happened to Gorgeous George?,* p. 20.

39   *"Many a time I lay in bed":* Ted Shane, "Gorgeous George The Wrestler," *American Mercury,* July 1950.

41   Jares provides most of the details about Gorgeous George, such as his dancing with Burt Lancaster, his walking barefoot in money, and his death. Thesz also paints a vivid picture of the man and the times, pp. 11–23.

41   *"We were free and independent":* Thesz, pp. 16, 172.

42   Information about the DuMont network and its pioneering of professional wrestling broadcasts comes from Michael

Ritchie's *Please Stand By: A Prehistory of Television* (Woodstock, NY: The Overlook Press, 1994).

42    *"If personality is an unbroken series of successful gestures":* F. Scott Fitzgerald, *The Great Gatsby* (New York: Scribners, 1925), p. 2.

43    *"cure weak men suffering from Lost Manhood":* National Police Gazette, February 18, 1893.

44    John F. Kasson describes the masculine reclamation projects at the turn of the century in his excellent *Houdini, Tarzan and the Perfect Man.*

44    *"I do not think I'm gorgeous":* Jares, p. 11.

### CHAPTER THREE: THE RAW AND THE COOKED

47    *"They look not only for more entertainment, but":* An 1857 letter Melville wrote to Clara Fisher Maeder, included in Maeder's *Autobiography* (ed. Douglas Taylor; New York, 1897).

49    *"every last vestige of the ancient human heritage of ritual":* Joseph Campbell, *The Hero with a Thousand Faces,* pp. 387–88.

50    a chance to be *"made free, for the time, by violence":* Gore Vidal, *The City and the Pillar* (New York: E.P. Dutton & Company, 1948), p. 34.

50    *"one of the most overlooked arenas":* Katherine Hansen and Anne McAuliffe, "Gender and Violence: Implications for Peaceful Schools," www.edc.org/womensequity/article/gbv.peace (no longer available).

50    *"playing on teams for the sheer joy of playing":* Marie Wilson, president of the Ms. Foundation for Women, in a memo calling for a nationwide "Son's Day," March 29, 1996. The event never occurred.

50    *"those who feel excluded from the modern world":* Lewis Mumford, *Art and Technics,* p. 53.

52    Roland Barthes, "The World of Wrestling," *Mythologies,* pp. 17, 20. (I resisted the temptation to quote lavishly from Barthes,

but his 1952 essay is indispensable reading. Long before Vince McMahon outed the business as "sports entertainment," Barthes said the obvious: that wrestling was pure theater, no different than a production of Racine. More important, he cut right through any highbrow disdain for popular and avowedly plebian activities. The essay was a breakthrough in cultural criticism.)

53    *"It is life itself"*: Mikhail Bakhtin, *Rabelais and His World,* p. 7.

54    *"a ridicule fused with rejoicing"*: Mikhail Bakhtin, *Problems of Dostoevsky's Poetics,* trans. Caryl Emerson (Manchester: Manchester University Press, 1984), p. 125.

55    Alexis de Tocqueville, *Democracy in America,* pp. 572, 575.

56    David Grimstead's *Melodrama Unveiled* and Lawrence Levine's *Highbrow/Lowbrow* describe the carnival atmosphere of the nineteenth-century American theater. They also provide vivid accounts of the cultural wars precipitating the Astor Place Riot. Levine quotes *Harper's* editor George William Curtis ("the biceps aesthetics": p. 57), Henry James ("instinctive hostility": p. 225), and George Templeton Strong ("nob and snob": p. 85). Michael Kammen's *American Culture, American Tastes* also provides useful context.

56    *Catering to the carousing bachelor class in the big cities: A Brief History of American Sports* by Elliot J. Gorn and Warren Goldstein provides a lively and intelligent introduction to game playing in America. Gorn's *The Manly Art* is also superb.

57    *"rowdyism, villainy, scoundrelism and boiled-down viciousness"*: Gorn quotes the *New York Tribune* (October 22, 1858) in *The Manly Art,* p. 120.

58    *dozens of small promotions throughout the United States:* The wrestling business has always been loosely organized. Histories are anecdotal and seldom completely reliable. I met many people devoted to collecting wrestling lore; my sense of the evolution of the business is gleaned mostly from conversations that never rose to the level of a question-and-

answer interview. Tom Burke and J. Michael Kenyon were particularly helpful. Lou Albano and Bert Sugar's *The Complete Idiot's Guide to Professional Wrestling*, Nat Fleischer's *From Milo to Londos,* Marcus Griffin's *Fall Guys,* Joe Jares's *Whatever Happened to Gorgeous George?,* and Lou Thesz's *Hooker* are necessary reading.

59    Vince McMahon describes his upbringing in a *Playboy* interview (February 2001). I quote from that article and from the *Current Biography Yearbook 1999.*

60    Shaun Assael and Mike Mooneyham's *Sex, Lies, and Headlocks* focuses on the last three decades of competition between Ted Turner (and WCW) and Vince McMahon (and WWE).

61    *with 20/20's John Stossel getting slapped upside the head:* Sharon Mazer has an insightful reading of the incident in *Professional Wrestling,* pp. 155–59.

64    Antonin Artaud, *Selected Writings* (ed. Susan Sontag; New York: Farrar, Straus & Giroux, 1976).

64    Tod Gordon told me about the Florida and Foley-Funk matches.

65    Assael and Mooneyham describe WWE's legal troubles and the response from WCW, pp. 84–161.

67    WWE's ratings: Nielsen Media Research. WWE's earnings are reported in the company's corporate disclosures. Newspaper and magazine interest is derived from LexisNexis. That the McMahons are billionaires: this has been reported in virtually every profile I have read about the couple.

CHAPTER FOUR: ACTION FIGURES OF SPEECH

69    *"Who knows in this life of ours what is really true":* Daniel Boorstin quotes Gabor in *The Image,* p. 161.

71    *"What it does is what, for other peoples with other temperaments":* Clifford Geertz, "Deep Play," *The Interpretation of Cultures,* p. 443.

72    *"the average, the bodily, the concrete, the democratic, the popular":*
      Walt Whitman, "Democratic Vistas" *Poetry and Prose* (New
      York: Library of America, 1982) p. 994.

72    *Folk art was one thing:* In his famous "Avant-Garde and Kitsch"
      essay, Clement Greenberg belittles popular culture and
      praises folk art, *Art and Culture,* p. 10.

72    *"ignoramuses":* From Macdonald's "Masscult & Midcult"
      essay in *Against the American Grain,* p. 18. The Mary Mc-
      Carthy quote comes from a prospectus she wrote for a jour-
      nal that never came to fruition, p. 66.

73    T. S. Eliot, "Marie Lloyd" (1923), *Selected Essays* (New York:
      Harcourt, Brace & World, 1964). Irving Howe, "Notes on
      Mass Culture" (1948), p. 498; Robert Warshow, "Paul, The
      Horror Comics, and Dr. Wertham" (1954); Leslie A. Fiedler,
      "The Middle Against Both Ends" (1955), p. 544, collected in
      *Mass Culture.*

73    *"Art is what you can get away with":* Andy Warhol, *The Philoso-
      phy of Andy Warhol: From A to B and Back Again* (New York:
      Harcourt Brace Jovanovich, 1975), pp. 54–55.

74    *the right things at the right time in the right way to the right people:*
      I've taken this idea and locution from Dick Hebdige's analy-
      sis of the British punk movement, *Subculture,* p. 122.

74    *ballet, "absurd by nature":* Edwin Denby, "Ballet: The American
      Position," *Dance Writings* (New York: Knopf, 1986), p. 507.

75    Shaun Assael and Mike Mooneyham's *Sex, Lies, and Headlocks*
      and Dave Meltzer's *Tributes* tell the story of Brian Pillman's
      rise and fall.

77    In a *Houston Chronicle* story about the deaths of the Von Erich
      sons (June 13, 1993) Evan Moore mentions the popularity of
      World Class Championship Wrestling in Israel.

77    Juan Forero reports on lady wrestlers in Bolivia, *New York
      Times,* July 21, 2005.

77   *"the structuring metaphor of the American experience"*: Richard Slotkin, *Regeneration Through Violence: The Mythology of the American Frontier, 1600–1860* (New York: HarperPerennial, 1996), p. 5.

78   *"sit in the stands . . . and acclaim others"*: Frederick Exley, *A Fan's Notes* (New York: Vintage, 1988), p. 134.

79   *"lacking in enough man's work"*: Paul Goodman, *Growing Up Absurd*, p. 12.

79   Susan Faludi chronicles the 1990s men's movement in *Stiffed*, pp. 224–88.

79   Robert Bly, *Iron John: A Book About Men*, pp. ix, x, 6, 36, 24.

CHAPTER FIVE: MANCHILD IN THE PROMISED LAND

83   *"To give to men that portion of hope"*: I found Lesueur's quote in Gustave Le Bon's *The Crowd*, p. 101.

83   *"One day," The Rock would tell himself*: Dwayne Johnson, *The Rock Says . . .* , p. 101.

84   *living in the "old, primitive, royal, animal way"*: Jack London, "A Piece of Steak," *Novels and Stories* (New York: Library of America, 1982), p. 853.

84   *the seven million households that did regularly watch the Monday night wrestling broadcasts:* That was in 1999 and 2000, when WWE and WCW were both broadcasting and popularity was keen.

84   *liked to get "camouflaged up, lock and load"*: Jesse Ventura, *I Ain't Got Time to Bleed,* pp. 133, 137.

85   *"excrement as worthy of their attention"*: George W. S. Trow, *Within the Context of No Context,* p. 56.

85   *"how things really are"*: Harry G. Frankfurt, *On Bullshit,* p. 30.

86   *"Of all Americans, only they are complete"*: Trow, p. 9.

95   The parenthetical quotations were collated from the following wrestlers' autobiographies: "I was down but not out,"

Bill Goldberg, *I'm Next,* p. 3; "I knew in my heart": Johnson, *The Rock Says . . . ,* p. 119; "there was a force guiding my life": Jesse Ventura, *I Ain't Got Time to Bleed,* p. 98; "I was getting so used to people calling me stupid": Mick Foley, *Mankind: Have a Nice Day,* p. 120; "Whatever it took": Johnson, p. 121; "I was meant to be somebody else": Joanie Laurer, *Chyna: If They Only Knew,* p. 9; "rich, successful, and the recipient of more ass": Foley, p. 48; "Don't think you gonna make a living": Foley, p. 66; "I had no desire to be some": Goldberg, p. 23; "I've got to defy death occasionally": Ventura, p. 169; "So that was how I got into drugs": Tom Billington, *Pure Dynamite,* p. 29; "If it's to be": Lou Thesz, *Hooker,* p. 22; "I am an object of": Laurer, p. 211; "Now I see it for what it was": Billington, p. 121; "What better training is there": Ventura, p. 163.

100 *From the dawn of humanity, boys have undergone elaborate tests and trials:* David D. Gilmore's cross-cultural *Manhood in the Making* explains and illustrates male rites of passage; it includes an introduction to Thomas Gregor's study of the Mehinaku Indians.

101 Norman Mailer is worth quoting in full here: "Masculinity is not something given to you, something you're born with, but something you gain. And you gain it by winning small battles with honor. Because there is very little honor left in American life, there is a certain built-in tendency to destroy masculinity in American men": *Cannibals and Christians* (New York: Dell, 1966), p. 201.

## CHAPTER SIX: CALIFORNIA DREAMING

107 *"My heart yearned to be known and loved":* Mary Shelley, *Frankenstein,* p. 116.

109 *"kayfabe," a language that old-school wrestlers learned from carneys:* Today kayfabe is largely mythic. I never heard a single wrestler, young or old, use it, and I doubt that any of them would know how.

DAVE MELTZER, THE MOST PRODUCTIVE WRITER IN AMERICA

117  *In 1979, it was psychiatrist Christopher Lasch's diagnosis: The Culture of Narcissism.*

117  *"remaking, remodeling, elevating and polishing one's very Self":* Tom Wolfe, "The Me Decade and the Third Great Awakening," *Mauve Gloves & Madmen, Clutter & Vine* (New York: Farrar, Straus and Giroux, 1976), p. 133.

117  *"In democratic communities, each citizen is habitually engaged":* Alexis de Tocqueville, *Democracy in America,* p. 596.

118  *"what do I do that I am most proud of":* Tom Peters, "Brand You," *Fast Company,* August/September 1997.

119  *Time was, one had to take enormous risk:* Daniel Boorstin chronicles the evolution of fame and celebrity in *The Image.*

119  *"represented a new democratic midget":* Leo Braudy tells the story of Charles S. Stratton's celebrity as General Tom Thumb in *The Frenzy of Renown,* pp. 498–506.

119  *"needn't have done—needn't do—anything special":* James Monaco, *Celebrity* (New York: Delta, 1978), p. 6.


CHAPTER SEVEN: MALE PERFORMANCE ANXIETY

127  *"You have a product":* Cited in Michael Kimmel's *Manhood in America,* p. 200.

127  *"a spectacle of excess":* Roland Barthes, "The World of Wrestling," *Mythologies,* p. 15.

128  *"You might as well ask me if I beat my wife":* Ted Shane, "Gorgeous George The Wrestler," *American Mercury,* July 1950.

128  *The wrestler David Shultz had a more succinct response:* ABC-TV, *20/20,* February 21, 1985.

128  *"I beat this guy!":* Joanie Laurer, *Chyna: If They Only Knew,* pp. 252–53.

129  *"Society is telling them now, more than ever before":* Harrison Pope et al., *The Adonis Complex,* p. 4.

128 *"I wanted to be more than a gimmick":* Laurer, in an October 2001 telephone interview.

132 *breathlessly touting the freedom, flexibility and self-affirming benefits:* Daniel H. Pink, "Free Agent Nation" *Fast Company,* December 1997.

132 *"everyone is a star":* Jedediah Purdy, in *For Common Things: Irony, Trust, and Commitment in America Today* (New York: Knopf, 1999), says that the phrase "We are as gods" is one of *Wired* editor Kevin Kelly's favorite slogans, p. 34.

141 Roddy Piper explained "the sickness" in a January 2002 interview; he also dilates on the pathologies of professional wrestling in his autobiography, *In the Pit with Piper,* chapter 12.

142 *"The one thing a woman cannot do":* Something a porn producer tells Susan Faludi in *Stiffed,* p. 543.

144 *"mastering the art of self-presentation":* Faludi, p. 531.


CHAPTER EIGHT: OBJECT LESSONS

147 *"I am my own commodity":* I found this remark in the program notes to an exhibit at the Museum of Modern Art, *Fame: After Photography* (New York, 1999). I believe Taylor said this when she launched her own line of perfume.

148 *men playing at being men:* The psychoanalyst Louise J. Kaplan terms this exaggerated emphasis on one's gender "homeovestism," an inverse of transvestism, disguising—instead of revealing—an urge to cross gender lines, *Female Perversions: The Temptations of Emma Bovary* (New York: Doubleday, 1991), pp. 237–83.

149 The 1990 documentary *Paris Is Burning,* directed by Jennie Livingston, explains the term "over" in the drag scene.

150 *"I want people to notice me":* Holly Brubach, *Girlfriend,* p. 47.

150 The details of Dwayne Johnson's football and wrestling career, as well as quotations separate from my April 2002 interview, are drawn from his autobiography, *The Rock Says . . .*, pp. 100, 112, 113.

151 *"One day we crave for mere subsistence":* Fleischer, *From Milo to Londos,* p. 289.

152 *"One day you're getting the adulation of the crowd":* Dwayne Johnson said in an interview.

152 Johnson on training with his father and joining WWE: *The Rocks Says . . .*, pp. 115–36.

154 *"He is the human pseudo-event":* Daniel Boorstin, *The Image,* pp. 57–58.

158 *"I just want to play me":* Susan Faludi, *Stiffed,* p. 583.

160 *"It was one of the most mindless things I have ever seen":* Bob Costas interviewing Vince McMahon for his HBO show *On the Record,* March 2001.

160 *"The critics who are saying we will never be able to do this":* Jere Longman, "The Finest Football February Can Offer," *New York Times,* February 12, 2001.

CHAPTER NINE: TOUGH LOVE

163 *"Do I have to arm wrestle you":* John Lennon, interviewed in *Newsweek,* October 1978.

163 *"Keep on bragging, keep on sassing, and always be outrageous":* David Remnick, *The King of the World* (New York: Vintage, 1998), p. 120.

164 Lou Thesz on Gorgeous George, *Hooker,* pp. 98–100.

164 *"It's a very gay sport":* Vadim, "Grappling with Homosexuality," *Village Voice,* May 9, 2000.

165 *"a laid-back cat . . . my fantasy creation":* Mick Foley, *Mankind: Have a Nice Day,* p. 48.

165 *"slammed, hip-tossed and suplexed without mercy":* Ibid., p. 69.

166 *"Wrestling was something I wanted to keep just to myself":* Ibid., p. 78.

166 *It has since "come out of the closet":* Dwayne Johnson, *The Rock Says . . . ,* p. 277.

166 *"their fetish":* Ibid., p. 277.

166 *"a big double rock burger with extra rock sauce on the side":* Ibid., p. 169.

166 *"Instead of shoving it down Stone Cold Steve Austin's throat":* Ibid., p. 169.

166 *"The average man needs at least a week to recover":* Ibid., p. 169.

166 *"I trusted him and he trusted me":* Ibid., p. 242.

166 *"Did Stone Cold Steve Austin Give The Rock all he could handle?":* Ibid., p. 260.

167 *"The door flew open and in walked Steve Austin":* Ibid., p. 261.

168 *"Get her out of the building":* Sharon Mazer, *Professional Wrestling,* p. 140.

168 *"Yes, I've got lust":* Ibid., p. 112.

172 *homosexual lovers were considered the ideal warriors:* Leo Braudy discusses the fighting prowess of homosexual soldiers in *From Chivalry to Terrorism,* pp. iv, x, 209–10.

173 *"if you can handle the largest arms in the world":* Mazer, p. 112.

173 *"It's very much like dancing":* Jesse Ventura, *I Ain't Got Time to Bleed,* p. 120.

174   *"it's kind of like being in bed with a young lady":* Dick Breyer interviewed for *Wrestling with the Past,* a series produced by John Dolin for Canadian television.

174   Dr. James Gilligan's *Violence* suggested my interpretation of the hostility rituals in professional wrestling. Formerly the director of the Bridgewater State Hospital for the criminally insane, Gilligan argues persuasively that shame—of feeling weak, of wanting love, of simply feeling ashamed—is the fundamental cause of all violence.

176   *"In naïve, or pure, Camp the essential element is seriousness":* Susan Sontag, "Notes on 'Camp,' " *Against Interpretation,* p. 283.

176   *"Camp is playful, anti-serious":* Ibid., p. 288.

176   *"expressing what's basically serious to you in terms of fun":* Christopher Isherwood, *The World in the Evening* (New York: Random House, 1954), p. 110.

176   *"exquisite mayhem":* I have taken this phrase from the title of Theo Ehret's exquisitely weird book *Wrestling and Girlie Photographs* (Cologne, Germany: Taschen, 2001).

176   *"What he learns is what his culture's ethos and his private sensibility":* Geertz, "Deep Play," *The Interpretation of Cultures,* p. 449.


CHAPTER TEN: PASSION PLAY

179   *"we are crude and sorrowful":* Erich Maria Remarque, *All Quiet on the Western Front* (trans. A. W. Wheen; New York: Fawcett, 1929), p. 123.

180   *the important thing is to prove that you could take a beating:* In *Manhood in the Making,* David Gilmore explains the importance of wounds and suffering in manhood rituals.

180   *"You just want to make them happy":* Pat Jordan, "Dysfunction for Dollars," *New York Times Magazine,* July 28, 2002.

185   *"Maybe self-improvement isn't the answer":* Chuck Palahniuk, *Fight Club,* p. 49.

185 *"We are the middle children of history"*: Ibid., p. 166.

187 *"Pain can be a cause of delight"*: Edmund Burke, *Philosophical Inquiry into the Sublime and Beautiful and Other Pre-Revolutionary Writings* (London: Penguin Classics, 1998), pp. 164, 127.


CHAPTER ELEVEN: A WORLD OF HURT

191 *"Whoever fights monsters"*: Friedrich Nietzsche, *Beyond Good and Evil: Prelude to a Philosophy of the Future* (trans. Walter Kaufmann; New York: Vintage, 1989), p. 146.

191 Material on the Von Erich family mostly comes from Dave Meltzer's *Tributes*, pp. 63–79. Karen Rouse calls Adkisson (Fritz Von Erich) "Godly" in a front-page obituary for the *Fort Worth Star-Telegram* (September 14, 1997). Evan Moore, writing for the *Houston Chronicle*, describes the brothers as "utterly American" in a June 13, 1993, account of their deaths. Steve Slagle describes the brothers as "an unstoppable juggernaut of youth," and Kerry as a "Hercules" in the online "Professional Wrestling Hall of Fame."

193 Quotations related to the death of Owen Hart come from Shaun Assael and Mike Mooneyham's *Sex, Lies, and Headlocks*, pp. 1–5.

194 Assael and Mooneyham provide an account of Owen Hart's funeral, Ibid., pp. 219–21.

195 *"I just found his death very moving"*: The quotes from fans are from the *Calgary Herald*'s extensive coverage of Owen Hart's death and funeral, May 31, 1999.

198 I picked up much of the background information about Stu Hart and his family during two visits to Calgary. Marsha Erb's *Stu Hart* provided many helpful details.

199 "STU HART GETS GALS IN A FLUSTER": Erb, pp. 83–84.

201 *"I'll always be a hero"*: From Paul Jay's excellent documentary *Hitman Hart: Wrestling with Shadows* (1998), which chronicles Bret Hart's difficult last days with WWE.

203 The trial of Lionel Tate received much attention in the media. For my account, I relied on reporting in the *Fort Lauderdale Sun-Sentinel*, the *New York Times*, the *Miami Herald*, and the *Palm Beach Post*, as well as conversations with Dr. Joel Klass and an attorney initially involved in defending Lionel's lawyer in a defamation suit brought by WWE. The suit claimed that Lionel's lawyer, as well as L. Brent Bozell, chairman of the Parents Television Council and its parent organization, the Media Research Center, had defamed WWE in blaming the deaths of four children, including Tiffany Eunick, on the violent nature of WWE's broadcasts. After U.S. District Court Judge Denny Chin of New York refused to dismiss the suit (*New York Law Journal*, May 31, 2001), the defendants settled by paying WWE $3.5 million in damages. In December 2003, Lionel Tate's life sentence was overturned. However, a year and a half after pleading guilty to second-degree murder and given a ten-year probation, he was arrested and charged with armed robbery of a pizza deliveryman in May 2005. If convicted, his life sentence may be reinstated.

207 Erb mentions Stu Hart's nickname for his oldest son, Smith, p. 169.

210 Meltzer gave Davey Boy Smith's troubled life and early death thorough coverage in the May 27 and June 3, 2002, issues of his *Wrestling Observer Newsletter*.

CHAPTER TWELVE: FINISHING MOVES

215 *"We are all in the gutter"*: Oscar Wilde, *Lady Windemere's Fan*, act III.

216 *"life itself is a dramatically enacted thing"*: Erving Goffman, *The Presentation of Self in Everyday Life*, p. 72.

218 *"There's a difference between":* Jerry Caggiano, vice president and creative director at Chicago-based Leo Burnett advertising agency (Tim Jones, "Military Sees No Rush to Enlist," *Chicago Tribune,* March 24, 2002). *The New York Times* quotes Secretary of the Army Louis Caldera on the "me-now" ethos (January 10, 2001). Eight months later—a week before 9/11—Caldera's successor, Thomas White, proclaimed the "Army of One" ad campaign a success. Later, however, "due to the realities of war," as a Pentagon personnel officer put it (*The New York Times,* July 24, 2005), the military was again struggling to meet recruiting goals.

225 *"frees human consciousness":* Bakhtin, *Rabelais and His World,* p. 49.

225 *nothing counters "the mockeries of the world" like laughter:* Ibid., p. 38.

228 *Laid up after a motorcycle accident:* Okay, I wasn't riding a Harley; it was a motor scooter, like a Vespa. Still . . .

228 *Wrestling seemed the perfect metaphor:* see, for instance, the *New York Times Book Review* cover illustration on the disputed 2000 presidential election, April 1, 2001.

232 *"I'm going to take over the world":* Shaun Assael and Mike Mooneyham, *Sex, Lies, and Headlocks,* p. 20.

233 *"his ratings began to sag":* In 2004, viewership was about half what it was four years earlier.

234 *the United States Justice Department charged Zicari and his wife with obscenity:* In January 2005, in a forty-five-page decision, U.S. District Judge Gary Lancaster dismissed the Justice Department's ten-count indictment against Rob Zicari and his wife, Janet Romano. Attorney General Alberto Gonzalez has said he will appeal the decision.

Albano, Lou, and Bert Randolph Sugar. *The Complete Idiot's Guide to Pro Wrestling*. New York: Alpha, 1999.

Angle, Kurt (with John Harper). *It's True! It's True!* New York: Regan Books, 2001.

Assael, Shaun, and Mike Mooneyham. *Sex, Lies, and Headlocks: The Real Story of Vince McMahon and the World Wrestling Federation*. New York: Crown, 2002.

Bakhtin, Mikhail. *Rabelais and His World* (trans. Hélene Iswolsky). Bloomington: Indiana University Press, 1984.

Barthes, Roland. *Mythologies* (trans., Annette Lavers). New York: Vintage, 1993.

Baudrillard, Jean. *Simulations* (trans., Paul Foss, Paul Patton, and Philip Beitchman). New York: Semiotext[e], 1983.

Bettleheim, Bruno. *The Uses of Enchantment: The Meaning and Importance of Fairy Tales*. New York: Vintage, 1977.

Billington, Tom. *Pure Dynamite: The Price You Pay for Wrestling Stardom*. Etobicoke, Ontario: Winding Stair, 2001.

Bly, Robert. *Iron John: A Book About Men.* Reading, MA: Addison-Wesley, 1990.

Boortstin, Daniel. *The Image: A Guide to Pseudo-Events in America.* New York: Vintage, 1992.

Braudy, Leo. *The Frenzy of Renown: Fame and Its History.* New York: Oxford University Press, 1986.

———. *From Chivalry to Terrorism: War and the Changing Nature of Masculinity.* New York: Knopf, 2003.

Brubach, Holly. *Girlfriend: Men, Women, and Drag.* New York: Random House, 2000.

Buford, Bill. *Among the Thugs.* New York: Vintage Departures, 1993.

Caillois, Roger. *Man, Play and Games* (trans., Meyer Barash). Urbana, IL: University of Illinois Press, 2001.

Campbell, Joseph. *Hero with a Thousand Faces.* New York: Meridian, 1956.

Canetti, Elias. *Crowds and Power* (trans., Carol Stewart). New York: Continuum, 1973.

Carter, Angela. "Giants' Playtime," in *Shaking a Leg: Journalism and Writings.* London: Chatto & Windus, 1997.

Debord, Guy. *Society of the Spectacle.* Detroit: Black & Red, 1983.

Dyer, Richard. *Heavenly Bodies: Film Stars and Society.* London: British Film Institute, 1986.

Ehret, Theo. *Exquisite Mayhem.* Cologne, Germany: Taschen, 2001.

Erasmus, Desiderius. *The Praise of Folly* (Hoyt Hopewell Hudson). Princeton, NJ: Princeton University Press, 1941.

Erb, Marsha. *Stu Hart: Lord of the Ring.* Toronto: ECW Press, 2002.

Faludi, Susan. *Stiffed: The Betrayal of the American Man.* New York: Morrow, 1999.

Fiske, John. *Understanding Popular Culture.* New York: Routledge, 1989.

Fleisher, Nat. *From Milo to Londos: The Story of Wrestling Through the Ages.* New York: Press of C. J. O'Brien, 1936.

Foley, Mick. *Have a Nice Day.* New York: Regan Books, 1999.

———. *Foley Is Good: And the Real World Is Faker Than Wrestling.* New York: HarperTorch, 2002.

———. *Tietam Brown.* New York: Knopf, 2003.

Frankfurt, Harry G. *On Bullshit.* Princeton, NJ: Princeton University Press, 2005.

Freud, Sigmund. *On Dreams* (1901; trans., James Strachey). New York: Norton, 1952.

———. "A Child Is Being Beaten" (1919), in *Sexuality and the Psychology of Love,* ed. Philip Rieff. New York: Collier, 1963.

———. *Beyond the Pleasure Principle* (1920; trans., James Strachey). New York: Norton, 1961.

———. *Group Psychology and the Analysis of the Ego* (1921; trans., James Strachey). New York: Norton, 1959.

———. "Medusa's Head" (1922), in *Sexuality and the Psychology of Love,* ed. Philip Rieff. New York: Collier, 1963.

———. *The Ego and the Id* (1923; trans., Joan Riviere; revised and ed., James Strachey). New York: Norton, 1961.

———. "Fetishism" (1927), in *Sexuality and the Psychology of Love,* ed. Philip Rieff. New York: Collier, 1963.

———. *Civilization and Its Discontents* (1930; trans., James Strachey). New York: Norton, 1961.

Gabler, Neal. *Life: The Movie: How Entertainment Conquered Reality.* New York: Knof, 1999.

Gamson, Joshua. *Claims to Fame: Celebrity in Contemporary America.* Berkeley: University of California Press, 1994.

Gans, Herbert J. *Popular Culture and High Culture: An Analysis and Evaluation of Taste.* New York: Basic, 1974.

Garbarino, James. *Lost Boys: Why Our Sons Turn Violent and How We Can Save Them.* New York: Free Press, 1999.

Geertz, Clifford. "Deep Play: Notes on the Balinese Cockfight," in *The Interpretation of Cultures.* New York: Basic, 1973.

Gilligan, James, M.D. *Violence: Reflections on a National Epidemic.* New York: Vintage, 1996.

Gilmore, David D. *Manhood in the Making: Cultural Concepts of Masculinity.* New Haven: Yale University Press, 1990.

Goffman, Erving. *The Presentation of Self in Everyday Life.* New York: Anchor, 1959.

Goldberg, Bill (with Steve Goldberg). *I'm Next: The Strange Journey of America's Most Unlikely Superhero.* New York: Crown, 2000.

Goodman, Paul. *Growing Up Absurd.* New York: Vintage, 1956.

Gorn, Elliott J. *The Manly Art: Bare-Knuckle Prize Fighting in America.* Ithaca, NY: Cornell University Press, 1986.

Gorn, Elliott J., and Warren Goldstein. *A Brief History of American Sports.* New York: Hill and Wang, 1993.

Greenberg, Clement. "Avant-Garde and Kitsch" (1939), in *Art and Culture: Critical Essays.* Boston: Beacon, 1961.

Greenblatt, Stephen Jay. *Learning to Curse: Essays in Early Modern Culture.* London: Routledge, 1992.

Griffin, Marcus. *Fall Guys: The Barnums of Bounce: The Inside Story of the Wrestling Business, America's Most Profitable and Best Organized Professional Sport.* Chicago: Reilly & Lee, 1937.

Grimstead, David. *Melodrama Unveiled: American Theater and Culture, 1800–1850.* Berkeley: University of California Press, 1987.

MATT BURNS, AKA NICK MONDO

Guttmann, Allen. *From Ritual to Record: the Nature of Modern Sport.* New York: Columbia University Press, 1978.

Hebdige, Dick. *Subculture: The Meaning of Style.* London: Routledge, 2001.

Huizinga, Johan. *Homo Ludens: A Study of the Play Element in Culture.* Boston: Beacon, 1955.

Jacobs, Norman (ed.). *Culture for the Millions: Mass Media in Modern Society.* Boston: Beacon, 1964.

Jares, Joe. *Whatever Happened to Gorgeous George?* Englewood Cliffs, NJ: Prentice-Hall, 1974.

Jenkins, Henry. "Never Trust a Snake: WWF Wrestling as a Masculine Melodrama," in *Out of Bounds: Sports, Media, and the Politics of Identity* (ed., Aaron Baker and Todd Boyd). Bloomington: Indiana University Press, 1997.

Johnson, Dwayne (with Joe Layden). *The Rock Says: The Most Electrifying Man in Sports Entertainment.* New York: Regan Books, 2000.

Kammen, Michael. *American Culture, American Taste: Social Change in the 20th Century.* New York: Basic, 1999.

Kasson, John F. *Houdini, Tarzan, and the Perfect Man: The White Male Body and the Challenge of Modernity in America.* New York: Hill and Wang, 2001.

Kasson, Joy S. *Buffalo Bill's Wild West: Celebrity, Memory, and Popular History.* New York: Hill and Wang, 2000.

Kimmel, Michael. *Manhood in America.* New York: Free Press, 1996.

Kipnis, Laura. *Bound and Gagged: Pornography and the Politics of Fantasy in America.* Durham, NC: Duke University Press, 1999.

Klein, Naomi. *No Logo: Taking Aim at the Brand Bullies.* New York: Picador USA, 2000.

Koestenbaum, Wayne. *The Queen's Throat: Opera, Homosexuality, and the Mystery of Desire.* New York: Vintage, 1993.

———. *Jackie Under My Skin: Interpreting an Icon.* New York: Plume, 1996.

Lasch, Christopher. *The Culture of Narcissism: American Life in an Age of Diminishing Expectations.* New York: Warner, 1979.

Lasn, Kalle. *Culture Jam: How to Reverse America's Suicidal Consumer Binge—and Why We Must.* New York: Quill, 2000.

Laurer, Joanie. *Chyna: If They Only Knew.* New York: Regan Books, 2001.

Le Bon, Gustave. *The Crowd: A Study of the Popular Mind.* New York: Ballantine, 1969.

Levine, Lawrence W. *Highbrow/Lowbrow: The Emergence of Cultural Hierarchy in America.* Cambridge: Harvard University Press, 1990.

Lifton, Robert Jay. *The Protean Self: Human Resilience in an Age of Fragmentation.* New York: Basic, 1993.

Lorenz, Konrad. *On Aggression* (trans., Marjorie Kerr Wilson). New York: Bantam, 1966.

Luciano, Lynne. *Looking Good: Male Body Image in Modern America.* New York: Hill and Wang, 2001.

Macdonald, Dwight. *Against the American Grain: Essays on the Effects of Mass Culture.* New York: Da Capo, 1983.

Mazer, Sharon. *Professional Wrestling: Sport and Spectacle.* Jackson: University Press of Mississippi, 1998.

Meltzer, Dave. *Tributes: Remembering Some of the World's Greatest Wrestlers.* Etobicoke, Ontario: Winding Stair Press, 2001.

Mitroff, Ian I., and Warren Bennis. *The Unreality Industry: The Deliberate Manufacturing of Falsehood and What It Is Doing to Our Lives.* New York: Birch Lane Press, 1989.

Mumford, Lewis. *Art and Technics.* New York: Columbia University Press, 1952.

Oates, Joyce Carol. *On Boxing.* Hopewell, NJ: Ecco, 1994.

Palahniuk, Chuck. *Fight Club.* New York: Henry Holt/Owl, 1997.

Piper, Rowdy Roddy (with Robert Picarello). *In the Pit with Piper.* New York: Berkley Boulevard, 2002.

Pirandello, Luigi. *Six Characters in Search of an Author* (trans., Eric Bentley). New York: Signet Classic, 1998.

Pollack, William. *Real Boys: Rescuing Our Sons from the Myths of Boyhood.* New York: Henry Holt, 1998.

Pope, Harrison, Jr., Katharine A. Phillips, and Roberto Olivardia. *The Adonis Complex: The Secret Crisis of Male Body Obsession.* New York: Free Press, 2000.

Postman, Neil. *Amusing Ourselves to Death: Public Discourse in the Age of Show Business.* New York: Penguin, 1986.

Pronger, Brian. *The Arena of Masculinity: Sports, Homosexuality, and the Meaning of Sex.* New York: St. Martin's, 1990.

Rosenberg, Bernard, and David Manning White, eds. *Mass Culture: The Popular Arts in America.* New York: Free Press, 1957.

Savage, Jon. *England's Dreaming: Anarchy, Sex Pistols, Punk Rock, and Beyond.* New York: St. Martin's/Griffin, 2001.

Schickel, Richard. *Intimate Strangers: The Culture of Celebrity in America.* Chicago: Ivan R. Dee, 2000.

Shelley, Mary. *Frankenstein.* New York: Bantam, 1991.

Simpson, Mark. "Big Tits! Masochism and Transformation in Bodybuilding," in *Male Impersonators: Men Performing Masculinity.* New York: Routledge, 1994.

Sommers, Christiana Hoff. *The War Against Boys: How Misguided Feminism Is Harming Our Young Men.* New York: Simon & Schuster, 2000.

Sontag, Susan. "Notes on 'Camp' " (1964), in *Against Interpretation.* New York: Delta, 1966.

Sorkin, Michael. "Faking It," in *Watching Television* (ed., Todd Gitlin). New York: Pantheon, 1986.

Strong, Marilee. *A Bright Red Scream: Self-Mutilation and the Language of Pain.* New York: Penguin, 1998.

Thesz, Lou (with Kit Bauman). *Hooker: An Authentic Wrestler's Adventures Inside the Bizarre World of Professional Wrestling.* Seattle: Wrestling Channel Press, 2000.

Tiger, Lionel. *Men in Groups.* London: Panther, 1970.

Tocqueville, Alexis de. *Democracy in America* (trans., Henry Reeve). New York: Bantam Classics, 2000.

WRESTLER KEN SWEENY AND KEN SWEENY, JR.

Trow, George W. S. *Within the Context of No Context*. Boston: Little, Brown, 1981.

Twitchell, James B. *Carnival Culture: The Trashing of Taste in America*. New York: Columbia University Press, 1992.

Ventura, Jesse. *I Ain't Got Time to Bleed: Reworking the Body Politic from the Bottom Up*. New York: Signet, 2000.

Williams, Linda. *Hard Core: Power, Pleasure, and the Frenzy of the Visible*. Berkeley: University of California Press, 1999.

THOMAS HACKETT has been writing for magazines and newspapers for nearly twenty years. Born and raised in Eugene, Oregon, he began contributing "Talk of the Town" pieces while working as a messenger at *The New Yorker* and has since published articles and photographs in *Rolling Stone, GQ, New York* magazine, the *New York Times Magazine,* and the *New York Times*. He lives in New York City.